THE ALGAE HOUSE

ABOUT THE FIRST BUILDIN
A BIOREACTOR FAÇAD

SPLITTERWERK & ARUP (ED.)
HEMMRICH / BLASCHITZ / WURM

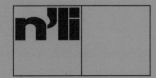

■ IDEA / CONCEPT / AUTHORSHIP: SPLITTERWERK, Label for Fine Arts and Engineering, Graz; Arup Deutschland GmbH, Berlin; B+G Ingenieure Bollinger und Grohman GmBH, Frankfurt; IMMOSOLAR GmbH, Hamburg ■ SPECIAL DISCIPLINES SPLITTERWERK, LABEL FOR FINE ARTS AND ENGINEERING "THE SMART TREEFROG": head of the competition team "Smart Material Houses", conception, design, architecture ■ PROJECT PARTNERS RESEARCH PROJECT SOLARLEAF – THE BIO-RESPONSIVE FAÇADE: SSC Strategic Science Consult GmbH, Colt International GmbH, Arup Deutschland GmbH ■ SPECIAL DISCIPLINES ARUP DEUTSCHLAND GMBH, RESEARCH PROJECT "SOLARLEAF – THE BIO-RESPONSIVE FAÇADE": project management, materials, building physics, façade design, building engineering, structural analysis of glass ■ SPECIAL DISCIP-LINES ARUP DEUTSCHLAND GMBH, BUILDING PROJECT "BIQ – THE ALGAE HOUSE – THE CLEVER TREEFROG": energy concept and simulation, building engineering, ICT (Information Communication Technology), structural analysis of glass ■ STAFF AT ARUP DEUTSCHLAND GMBH: Tobias Burkard, Graham Dodd, Andreas Ewert, Matthias Frechen, Yaiza Gonzales, Nicolo Guariento, Jan Jirak, Ewan McLeod, Marina Miceli, Sebastian Oehm, Martin Pauli, Dirk Regenspurger, Henning Schlechtriem, Rudi Scheuermann, Cornelius Schneider, Felix Weber, Jan Wurm, Gertraud Zwiens ■ STAFF AT COLT INTERNATIONAL GMBH: Lukas Verlage, Ulrich Kremer, Manfred Starlinger, Jörg Ribbecke, Markus Ticheloven ■ STAFF AT STRATEGIC SCIENCE CONSULT GMBH (SSC): Martin Kerner, Stefan Hindersin ■ SPECIAL DISCIPLINES SPLITTERWERK, LABEL FOR FINE ARTS AND ENGINEERING "THE CLEVER TREEFROG": conception, design, architecture, artistic direction ■ PROJECT TEAM SPLITTERWERK, LABEL FOR FINE ARTS AND ENGINEERING "THE CLEVER TREEFROG": Mark Blaschitz, Edith Hemmrich, Max Jüngling, Josef Roschitz, Ingrid Somitsch, Stephanie Wolf ■ PLANNING PART-NERS, HAMBURG: sprenger von der lippe; Timm & Goullon; Technisches Büro der Otto Wulff Bauunternehmung GmbH ■ CONSTRUCTION MANAGEMENT: Otto Wulff Bauunternehmung GmbH ■ CLIENT / INVESTOR: KOS Wulff Immobilien GmbH ■ CO-INVESTOR: SSC Strategic Science Consult GmbH ■ RESEARCH PROJECT "SOLARLEAF – DIE BIO-ADAPTIVE FASSADE" FUNDING: Research Initiative Zukunft Bau of the Federal Institute for Research on Building, Urban Affairs and Spatial Development (Bundesinstitut für Bau-, Stadt- und Raum-forschung) ■ BUILDING PROJECT "BIQ – THE ALGAE HOUSE – THE CLEVER TREEFROG" FUNDING: IBA Hamburg GmbH, Otto Wulff Bauunternehmung, Colt International GmbH, SSC Strategic Science Consult GmbH, Arup Deutschland GmbH, BGT Bischoff Glastechnik AG ■ PROJECT INITIATORS: International Building Exhibition Hamburg, IBA Hamburg GmbH

DAS ALGENHAUS

ÜBER DAS ERSTE GEBÄUDE MIT BIOREAKTORFASSADE

SPLITTERWERK & ARUP (HRSG.)
HEMMRICH / BLASCHITZ / WURM

CONTENTS

INHALT

OLAF SCHOLZ
■ WELCOME NOTE

■ FIRST MAYOR OF THE FREE AND HANSEATIC CITY OF HAMBURG

■ Developing renewable energy from wind, sun, biomass and geothermal sources is of crucial importance with regard to future energy supply. With a view to the Energy Transition, we rely on the creativity of architects and scientists in the spirit of modern urban development. The result can be seen on the site of the International Building Exhibition (IBA) in Hamburg. One example is the IBA project BIQ – better known as the Algae House – that generates its own energy with its algae bioreactor façade.

BIQ is the first building anywhere in the world equipped with this kind of façade, that is part of a holistic regenerative energy concept. It is one of the "Smart Material Houses" models with which the building exhibition demonstrated new and intelligent building materials for use in buildings and façades. In Hamburg we are pleased to have our city serve as the site for a particularly innovative building that has met with great acclaim not only among experts.

SIEGFRIED NAGL
■ WELCOME NOTE

■ MAYOR OF THE CITY OF GRAZ

■ Graz has been a UNESCO City of Design since 2011. For us this means that promoting education and culture, innovation and creativity takes top priority on the city's agenda.

SPLITTERWERK is one such innovative company. When we think about the global environmental situation, we should not wait for international conferences to agree guidelines, but simply act.

Around forty per cent of total final energy is consumed in buildings. It is therefore more urgent than ever before to reduce energy consumption by using new façade solutions so as to achieve Europe's energy and climate goals. After all, the best energy is energy which is not used.

Until recently, the main purpose of a façade in cities was to give a building a certain recognition value and to optimise integration into existing urban settings. Over the years, however, functional use of façades has become an increasingly important aspect.

The example of photo-bioreactors in the façade shows that new solutions can be created by combining and integrating existing advanced technologies.

It's not only the environment that benefits from new façade solutions, residents also experience an increase in the comfort factor thanks to automatic shading and temperature control mechanisms. So the algae house is a smart solution! To borrow an advertising slogan, I can only say "That's how technology must be". I wish the SPLITTERWERK team the best of success for their future work!

JUTTA BLANKAU
■ WELCOME NOTE

■ SENATOR FOR URBAN DEVELOPMENT AND THE ENVIRONMENT OF THE FREE AND HANSEATIC CITY OF HAMBURG

■ "BIQ – The Algae House" is an extraordinary project carried out as part of the International Building Exhibition (IBA) in Hamburg, Wilhelmsburg.

For me, the combination of cutting-edge building materials and pioneering energy concepts with housing is a glimpse of the future. In some projects, the themes of IBA Hamburg – climate change, urban development, and diverse urban society – are focused as if through a burning-glass. This is certainly the case with this residen-

OLAF SCHOLZ
□ GRUSSWORT

□ ERSTER BÜRGERMEISTER DER FREIEN UND HANSESTADT HAMBURG

□ Der Ausbau erneuerbarer Energien aus Wind, Sonne, aus Biomasse und Erdwärme ist für die Energieversorgung der Zukunft von zentraler Bedeutung. Mit Blick auf die Energiewende setzen wir im Sinne einer modernen Stadtentwicklung auf die Kreativität von Architekten und Wissenschaftlern. Das Resultat kann man in Hamburg auf dem Gelände der Internationalen Bauausstellung besichtigen. Dazu gehört auch das IBA-Projekt BIQ – besser bekannt unter dem Namen Algenhaus, das sich über seine Algen-Bioreaktorfassade selbst mit Energie versorgt.

BIQ ist weltweit das erste Gebäude mit einer solchen Fassade, die Teil eines ganzheitlich regenerativen Energiekonzepts ist. Es gehört zu den Modellen der „Smart Material Houses", mit denen die Bauausstellung neue und intelligente Baustoffe gezeigt hat, die in Gebäuden und Fassaden verwendet werden. Wir in Hamburg freuen uns, dass unsere Stadt Standort für ein besonders innovatives Gebäude ist, das nicht nur in der Fachwelt viel Beachtung findet.

SIEGFRIED NAGL
□ GRUSSWORT

□ BÜRGERMEISTER DER STADT GRAZ

□ Graz ist seit 2011 UNESCO City of Design. Das bedeutet für uns, dass die Förderung von Bildung und Kultur, von Innovation und Kreativität ganz oben auf der städtischen Agenda steht.

SPLITTERWERK ist so ein innovatives Unternehmen. Wenn wir an die globale Umweltsituation denken, sollten wir nicht auf Vorgaben von internationalen Konferenzen warten, sondern einfach handeln.

Rund 40 Prozent der gesamten Endenergie wird in Gebäuden verbraucht. Daher ist die Reduzierung des Energieverbrauchs mit dem Einsatz von neuen Fassadenlösungen notwendiger denn je, um die energie- und klimapolitischen Ziele Europas zu erreichen. Denn die beste Energie ist die nicht verbrauchte.

Bis vor Kurzem war die Hauptfunktion einer Fassade im urbanen Gebiet, dem Gebäude einen bestimmten Wiedererkennungswert zu geben und das Eingliedern in eine bestehende städtebauliche Gestaltung zu optimieren, doch über die letzten Jahre hat die funktionelle Verwendbarkeit der Fassade an Bedeutung gewonnen.

Das Beispiel der eingesetzten Photobioreaktoren in der Fassade zeigt, dass durch Verschmelzung von vorhandenen hochentwickelten Technologien und deren Integration neue Lösungen entstehen.

Nicht nur die Umwelt profitiert von neuen Fassadenlösungen, sondern auch für die Bewohner erhöht sich der Wohlfühlfaktor durch automatische und temperatursteuernde (Beschattungs-)Mechanismen. Das Algenhaus ist also eine smarte Lösung! In Anlehnung an einen Werbespruch kann ich nur sagen: „So muss Technik". Ich wünsche dem Team von SPLITTERWERK weiterhin viel Erfolg!

JUTTA BLANKAU
□ GRUSSWORT

□ SENATORIN FÜR STADTENTWICKLUNG UND UMWELT DER FREIEN UND HANSESTADT HAMBURG

□ Mit „BIQ – das Algenhaus" ist im Rahmen der Internationalen Bauausstellung (IBA) in Hamburg-Wilhelmsburg ein außerordentliches Projekt verwirklicht worden.

Die Verbindung von modernsten Baustoffen und wegweisenden energetischen Konzepten mit dem Thema Wohnen ist für mich ein Blick in die Zukunft. In manchen Projekten bündeln sich die Themen

tial building with its façade of photo-biocollectors. Not only does this demonstrate a combination of various sources of renewable energy, it also tries to find an answer to how living space can be flexibly adapted to the needs of its inhabitants.

Of course, "BIQ – The Algae House" is avant-garde. With its bioreactor façade and its energy concept, the building is a model for the future. I hope that many elements will be used in other building projects too, after all that is the whole point of pioneering projects of this kind.

We need good ideas about how we can reconcile affordable housing, high energy standards, and economic efficiency in new buildings and modernisation. Everyone should be able to benefit from this: tenants and building developers, landlords and owners, and of course the climate.

Projects such as the Algae House are important. They can demonstrate what the future of sustainable housing can be like.

JÖRN WALTER ■ RETHINKING ARCHITECTURE

■ SENIOR BUILDING DIRECTOR OF THE FREE AND HANSEATIC CITY OF HAMBURG

■ In view of energy-related and ecological challenges, we need to rethink architecture. SPLITTERWERK is among the few firms who tackle this issue fundamentally. One example is the "Algae House – The Clever Treefrog" that focuses rigorously on smart material: the bioreactor façade networks material and energy flows with intelligent building technology and also turns the role of the building shell, as a central element in energy exchange, into a provocative aesthetic formal principle. This approach is also reflected in the load-bearing structure and in the unconventional floor plans and furnishings. Here, architecture becomes a technological, social and aesthetic event in which visitors oscillate between discomfiture and fascination. It has opened the door to a space of possibility that can be further developed with "Supernature", if their courage does not fail them, and if building developers do not lose their willingness to take risks.

GUIDO HAGEL ■ WELCOME NOTE

■ COORDINATOR OF THE RESEARCH INITIATIVE FUTURE BUILDING AT THE FEDERAL INSTITUTE FOR RESEARCH ON BUILDING, URBAN AFFAIRS AND SPATIAL DEVELOPMENT

■ There is a broad consensus in society that we must use energy more efficiently and make greater use of renewables in energy supply. Buildings have vast potentials when it comes to reducing greenhouse gas emissions significantly and increasing the percentage of renewable energies in energy consumption. Developments in the building sector show what is possible even now.

One example is "BIQ – The Algae House – The Clever Treefrog", a building erected for the International Building exhibition in Hamburg. It is the world's first building to be equipped with a bioreactor façade. The façade elements are used to cultivate microalgae and to absorb solar thermal energy on the building's shell. The biomass produced by the microalgae and the solar heat supply the building with sufficient energy.

The façades were researched and developed with the financial support of the "Zukunft Bau" research initiative operated by the Federal Ministry for the Environment, Nature Conservation, Building and Nuclear Safety. The Federal Institute for Research on Building, Urban Affairs and Spatial Development is the project management agency for the initiative. The results of the research are impressive, a real-world system that is good for the climate.

der IBA Hamburg – Klimawandel, Stadtentwicklung und vielfältige Stadtgesellschaft – wie in einem Brennglas. Bei diesem Wohnhaus mit seiner Gebäudefassade aus Photobiokollektoren ist das der Fall. Nicht nur, dass hier exemplarisch die Kombination verschiedener Quellen erneuerbarer Energien praktiziert wird, es will auch eine Antwort darauf liefern, wie Wohn- und damit Lebensräume flexibel den Bedürfnissen der Bewohner angepasst werden können.

„BIQ – Das Algenhaus" ist natürlich Avantgarde. Es ist mit seiner Bioreaktorfassade und seinem Energiekonzept ein gebauter Zukunftsentwurf. Ich hoffe, dass später viele Elemente auch in anderen Bauvorhaben Verwendung finden, denn das ist der Sinn solcher Pionierprojekte.

Wir brauchen gute Ideen, wie wir bezahlbaren Wohnraum, einen hohen energetischen Standard und die Wirtschaftlichkeit bei Neubau und Modernisierung zusammenbringen können. Davon sollen alle profitieren: Mieter und Bauherren, Vermieter und Eigentümer und natürlich auch das Klima.

Projekte wie das Algenhaus sind wichtig. Sie können uns zeigen, wie die Zukunft des nachhaltigen Wohnens aussehen kann.

JÖRN WALTER □ ARCHITEKTUR NEU DENKEN

□ OBERBAUDIREKTOR DER FREIEN UND HANSESTADT HAMBURG

□ Vor dem Hintergrund der energetischen und ökologischen Herausforderungen muss Architektur neu gedacht werden. SPLITTERWERK gehört zu den wenigen Büros, die sich das Thema vom Grunde her zur Aufgabe gemacht und mit dem „Algenhaus – The Clever Treefrog" ein Beispiel umgesetzt haben, das smart material radikal ins Zentrum rückt: Die Bioreaktorfassade vernetzt die Material- und Energieströme mit intelligenter Gebäudetechnologie, erhebt die Rolle der Gebäudehülle als zentrales Element des Energieaustausches aber zugleich auch zum provokanten ästhetischen Gestaltungsprinzip. Das setzt sich in der Tragwerksstruktur sowie den unkonventionellen Grundrissen und der Möblierung fort. Architektur wird hier im besten Case-Study-Sinn technologisch, sozial und ästhetisch zu einem Ereignis, bei dem die Besucher zwischen Befremdung und Faszination hin- und herschwanken. Es wurde die Tür zu einem Möglichkeitsraum geöffnet, der mit „Supernature" noch weiterentwickelt werden kann, so der Mut sie nicht verlässt und Bauherren ihre Bereitschaft zum Wagnis nicht verlieren.

GUIDO HAGEL □ GRUSSWORT

□ KOORDINATOR FORSCHUNGSINITIATIVE ZUKUNFT BAU AM BUNDESINSTITUT FÜR BAU-, STADT- UND RAUMFORSCHUNG

□ Es ist ein breiter gesellschaftlicher Konsens, Energie effizienter zu nutzen und bei der Energieversorgung auf die Erneuerbaren zu setzen. In Gebäuden schlummern große Potenziale, wenn es darum geht, Treibhausgasemission deutlich zu reduzieren und den Anteil erneuerbarer Energien am Energieverbrauch zu steigern. Entwicklungen im Bauwesen zeigen, was schon jetzt alles möglich ist Ein Beispiel ist das Gebäude „BIQ – Das Algenhaus – The Clever Treefrog", das für die Internationale Bauausstellung in Hamburg gebaut wurde. Es ist das weltweit erste Haus mit einer Bioreaktorfassade. Die Fassadenelemente dienen der Kultivierung von Mikroalgen und der Aufnahme solarthermischer Energie an der Gebäudehülle Die Biomasse der Mikroalgen und die Sonnenwärme versorgen das Gebäude mit genügend Energie.

Erforscht und entwickelt wurden die Fassaden mit finanzieller Unterstützung der Forschungsinitiative Zukunft Bau des Bundesministeriums für Umwelt, Naturschutz, Bau und Reaktorsicherheit. Das Bur

I hope you enjoy reading this fascinating publication and that it will be a source of inspiration for your own ambitious projects.

ULI HELLWEG
■ WELCOME NOTE

■ CEO OF THE IBA HAMBURG

■ International building exhibitions are temporary, curated formats of urban development, town planning, and architecture. Unlike biennials, they last up to ten years, designed to bring about long-term structural change of their venue. As "laboratories", they have been dedicated to local issues for more than a hundred years in Germany. The result is conceptual and architectural projects whose quality garners international attention.

In 2013, in the final year of the IBA Hamburg show, around 460,000 guests from Germany and abroad visited Hamburg's Elbe islands and inland port to experience for themselves the innovative force of the projects carried out over the past seven years. The "Metrozones" theme demonstrates by way of example how inner-city peripheral areas can be developed. International urban society and its contribution to the growing city under educational and art projects are manifested in the "Cosmopolis" theme. The aim of the "Cities and Climate Change" project is to achieve energy and CO_2 neutrality of the Elbe island Wilhelmsburg. Energy-efficient buildings and decentralised energy networks play a key role in this context. The building itself becomes a bioreactor in the "BIQ – The Algae House – The Clever Treefrog" project. This has effects on technical fittings and, directly, on room layout.

"BIQ – The Algae House – The Clever Treefrog" by the SPLITTERWERK studio impressively demonstrates the symbiosis of infrastructure and shell. The algae façade binds CO_2, generates biomass, while at the same time producing heat for the building. Intelligent apartment typologies inside BIQ, for instance the "Milan" and "Hamburg" apartments, experiment with forward-looking flexible floor plans.

Biomass generated on façades opens up new perspectives for rural and urban regions. Instead of dedicating extensive rape and corn fields to the production of energy as opposed to food, it is possible for previously unused façades on warehouses, factories, office and residential buildings to make a substantial contribution to future local energy supply by means of bioreactor façades.

We would like to take this opportunity to thank everyone involved for the successful cooperation and hope that the publication meets with a positive response!

---

desinstitut für Bau-, Stadt- und Raumforschung ist Projektträger der Initiative. Die Ergebnisse der Forschung können sich sehen lassen. Entstanden ist ein praxistaugliches System, das gut fürs Klima ist. Ich wünsche Ihnen eine anregende Lektüre und Inspiration für eigene mutige Projekte.

ULI HELLWEG
□ GRUSSWORT

□ GESCHÄFTSFÜHRER DER IBA HAMBURG

□ Internationale Bauausstellungen sind temporäre, kuratierte Formate der Stadtentwicklung, des Städtebaus und der Architektur. Entgegen einer Biennale dauern sie bis zu zehn Jahre an und sind auf einen langfristigen strukturellen Wandel ihres Austragungsortes angelegt. Als „Labore" widmen sie sich in Deutschland seit über 100 Jahren lokalen Fragestellungen. Konzeptionelle und bauliche Projekte, deren Qualität internationale Aufmerksamkeit erfahren, resultieren darin.

2013, im finalen Präsentationsjahr der IBA Hamburg, besuchten circa 460.000 Gäste aus dem In- und Ausland Hamburgs Elbinseln und den Hamburger Binnenhafen, um sich von der Innovationskraft der in den vorangegangenen sieben Jahren umgesetzten Projekte zu überzeugen. Das Thema „Metrozonen" zeigt hier exemplarisch, wie man innerstädtische Peripherien entwickeln kann. Die Internationale Stadtgesellschaft und ihr Beitrag zur wachsenden Stadt im Rahmen von Bildungs- und Kunstprojekten manifestieren sich im Thema „Kosmopolis". Das Thema der „Stadt im Klimawandel" verfolgt das Ziel der Energie- sowie CO_2-Neutralität der Elbinsel Wilhelmsburg. Dabei spielen energieeffiziente Gebäude und dezentrale Energienetze eine besondere Rolle. Beim Projekt „BIQ – Das Algenhaus – The Clever Treefrog" wird das Gebäude selbst zum Bioreaktor. Das hat Auswirkungen auf die technische Ausstattung und unmittelbar auch auf die räumliche Organisation.

Das „BIQ – Das Algenhaus – The Clever Treefrog" vom Atelier SPLITTERWERK zeigt eindrucksvoll die Symbiose von Infrastruktur und Hülle. Die Algenfassade bindet CO_2, erzeugt Biomasse und produziert sogleich Wärme für das Gebäude. Intelligente Wohntypologien im Inneren des BIQ, wie die „Mailänder" und die „Hamburger" Wohnungen, experimentieren mit zukunftsweisenden flexiblen Grundrissen.

An Fassaden erzeugte Biomasse eröffnet neue Perspektiven für ländliche wie urbane Regionen. Statt große Raps- und Maisfelder der Energie- anstelle der Lebensmittelproduktion zu widmen, können bislang ungenutzte Fassaden von Lagerhallen, Fabriken aber auch Büro- und Wohngebäude durch Bioreaktorfassaden einen erheblichen Beitrag zur zukünftigen lokalen Energieversorgung leisten.

Wir möchten uns an dieser Stelle bei allen Akteuren für die erfolgreiche Zusammenarbeit bedanken und wünschen Ihnen viel positive Resonanz auf die vorliegende Publikation!

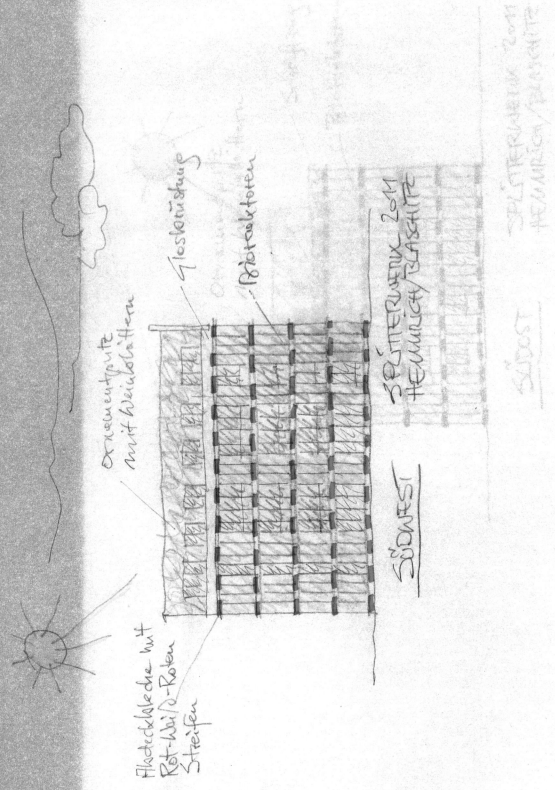

Ornamentputz mit Weinblättern

Glockenschlag

Aborakoten

Flachdecke mit Rot-Weiß-Roten Streifen

SÜDWEST

SPLITTERWERK 2011
HEINRICH RASCHITZ

SÜDOST

SPLITTERWERK 2011
HEINRICH RASCHITZ

EDITH HEMMRICH & MARK BLASCHITZ
■ PREFACE

■ COFOUNDERS AND OWNERS OF
THE SPLITTERWERK LABEL

At the beginning of February 2014 we were invited to present SPLITTERWERK's current works at the 14th Venice Architecture Biennale. We opted for our "Case Study House" with the world's first bioreactor façade, realised as part of the International Building Exhibition (IBA) Hamburg in 2013. In this context Arup and SPLITTERWERK developed this book titled "The Algae House".

The project for Hamburg has a long history and is the result of intensive interdisciplinary design and planning processes lasting several years and involving cultural studies scholars, visual artists, and engineers in teaching, research and business. Before SPLITTERWERK – together with seven other internationally well-known architectural firms – was invited in summer 2009 to take part in the "Smart Material House" competition held by the renowned specialist magazine arch+, our studio had already attracted a great deal of international attention with its prototypical buildings. It all began in 1986 with the "Wohnhügel", a competition proposal for a residential building in Graz. Long before the green façade trend took hold, the concept for the north façade of this strictly east-west facing building featured a "Green Wall". This front-mounted, self-supporting masonry structure was made up of dry stacking retaining blocks familiar from road construction. Unfortunately, the competition jury decided against our entry at the time. The first project actually built was the "Wohnstück" in 1992, a low-cost multi-storey prefab wood panel residential building with a soft curtain wall of wire-woven wood slats. These "slatted shades" for sun-shading walls and wall openings served as a trellis for vines (edible façade) and climbing plants of a wide range of different genera. Then came "Red Treefrog" (1993–1997) with a living sunshade, "Black Treefrog" (1998–2004) with wooden trellis as a building envelope, "The Smart Treefrog (2009–2011) with algae bioreactors as a climate envelope (↑ Fig. P. 18) and "The Clever Treefrog (2011–2013) with algae bioreactors as a curtain façade, five buildings that combined biology and technology in a differentiated manner to create intelligent architectural concepts. Plants and building elements were turned into units of design with an active effect in terms of buildings physics as part of an environment planned in a manner suitable for current times – a holistically sustainable cultural landscape of the 21st century.

For us, "Smart Buildings" are not traditional building typologies in which conventional building materials are replaced by "Smart Materials" so as to create a kind of "high-tech update" to an ordinary building with electronically controlled features for security, air-conditioning, household, and so on. "Smart Buildings" blaze a trail in terms of building theory, they make statements about the relationship between public, communal and private space, and zone a building according to specific requirements of use and air-conditioning. "Smart Buildings" are houses that can no longer be conceived, planned and assessed primarily in terms of results, but rather additionally demonstrate qualities in their suitability for processes. For example the timing of events in the home, changes in programme can define the appearance of an apartment in accordance with specific user requirements – the result are "Smart Spaces" with different typologies of reconfigurable floor plans within an envelope – a phenomenon which we call "Supernature", because it works similar to an artificial biosphere.

The development of "Smart Skins" can also be seen as being of great importance. The function of the skin of buildings is at least as important, complex and diverse as that of plants and animals. The building skin has a major impact on the energy balance, views (possible views in and out of the building) and the appearance of a

---

EDITH HEMMRICH & MARK BLASCHITZ
□ VORWORT

□ MITBEGRÜNDER UND EIGENTÜMER
DER MARKE SPLITTERWERK

□ Anfang Februar 2014 bekamen wir mit SPLITTERWERK eine Einladung anlässlich der 14. Architekturbiennale Venedig unsere aktuellen Arbeiten vorzustellen. Unsere Wahl fiel dabei auf das „Case-Study-House" mit der weltersten Bioreaktorfassade, realisiert im Rahmen der Internationalen Bauausstellung (IBA) Hamburg 2013. In diesem Zusammenhang entstand in Kooperation zwischen Arup und SPLITTERWERK die vorliegende Publikation „The Algae House" (Das Algenhaus).

Das Projekt für Hamburg hat eine lange Vorgeschichte und ist das Resultat intensiver und mehrjähriger transdisziplinärer Design- und Planungsprozesse zwischen Kulturwissenschafterinnen, Bildenden Künstlerinnen und Ingenieurinnen, tätig in Lehre, Forschung und Wirtschaft. Bevor SPLITTERWERK im Sommer 2009 zusammen mit sieben weiteren international bekannten Architekturbüros zum Wettbewerb „Smart Material House" vom renommierten Fachmagazin arch+ geladen wurden, konnte unser Atelier mit seinen prototypischen Gebäuderealisierungen bereits weltweit Aufmerksamkeit erregen. Begonnen hat alles bereits 1986 mit dem „Wohnhügel", ein Wettbewerbsvorschlag für einen Wohnbau in Graz. Lange vor dem Trend bewachsener Fassaden hat das Konzept für die Nordfassade des streng Ost-West ausgerichteten Baukörpers eine „Grüne Wand" vorgesehen. Diese vorgestellte und selbsttragende Mauerwerkskonstruktion wurde aus im Straßenbau bekannten Betonlöffelsteinen gebildet. Die Wettbewerbsjury entschied sich zu dieser Zeit leider gegen unseren Beitrag. Das erste realisierte Projekt war 1992 das „Wohnstück", ein Low-cost-Geschosswohnbau in Holztafelfertigbauweise mit einer weichen Vorhangfassade aus mit Draht verwobenen Holzlamellen. Diese sogenannten „Rollschatten" zur Wand- und Wandöffnungsbeschattung fungierten als Rankgerüst für Wein (essbare Fassade) und Kletterpflanzen unterschiedlichster Gattungen. Es folgten „Roter Laubfrosch" (1993–1997) mit lebendem Sonnenschutz, „Schwarzer Laubfrosch" (1998–2004) mit Rollschatten als Gebäudehülle, „The Smart Treefrog" (2009–2011) mit Algenbioreaktoren als Klimahülle (↑ Abb. S. 18) und „The Clever Treefrog" (2011–2013) mit Algenbioreaktoren als vorgehängte Fassade, fünf Projekte, die in differenzierter Weise Biologie und Technologie zu intelligenten architektonischen Konzepten miteinander verknüpfen. Pflanzen und Bauelemente wurden dabei zu gestalterisch und bauphysikalisch wirksamen und funktionierenden Einheiten als Teile einer zeitgemäß geplanten Umwelt – einer ganzheitlich nachhaltigen Kulturlandschaft des 21. Jahrhunderts.

„Smart Buildings" (intelligente Gebäude) sind für uns keine traditionellen Gebäudetypologien, bei denen herkömmliche Baumaterialien durch „Smart Materials" (intelligente Materialien) ersetzt werden und ein gewöhnliches Gebäude sozusagen ein „hightech-updating" erfährt bzw. elektronisch gesteuerte Features für Sicherheit, Klima und Haushalt etc. erhält. „Smart Buildings" haben eine zukunftsweisende Gebäudelehre, machen Aussagen zum Verhältnis zwischen öffentlich, gemeinschaftlich und privat und zonieren ein Gebäude nutzungsspezifisch und klimatisch. „Smart Buildings" sind Häuser, die nicht mehr nur vorrangig ergebnisorientiert erdacht, geplant und beurteilt werden können, sondern zusätzlich vielmehr die Qualitäten in ihrer Prozesstauglichkeit beweisen. So kann z.B. der zeitliche Wohnablauf, das wechselnde Programm userorientiert das Erscheinungsbild einer Wohnung prägen – es entstehen „Smart Spaces" (intelligente Räume) mit unterschiedlichen Typologien von re-konfigurierbaren Grundrissen innerhalb einer Gebäudehülle – von uns „Supernature" genannt, die ähnlich einer künstlichen Biosphäre funktioniert.

Auch der Entwicklung von „Smart Skins" (intelligenten Hüllen) kann eine hohe Bedeutung beigemessen werden. Die Funktion der Haut von Gebäuden ist mindestens genauso wichtig, komplex und vielfältig

building, for example. Because the skin is the interface between two spaces (e.g. interior and exterior), it makes sense to incorporate as many functional requirements in it as possible: it can be light-absorbing, reflective, opaque, translucent, transparent, photovoltaic, insulating, accumulating, self-lighting, many-coloured, controllable, passive, active, interactive and reversible, among other things. Today, "Smart Skins" still tend to be a complex combination of different building elements of a wide range of materials ("thick wall"). Alternating in their ratio to each other and catering for different demands, they make up the building's shell. In addition to materials and combinations of materials with supporting and room-forming functions and effects in terms of building physics, materials with a visual effect are also used. While "Smart Technologies" such as computer-controlled surfaces comprising LED and OLED have a purely visual effect, changes in colour, form and design of "Smart Materials" can be reversibly achieved by means of light, temperature, electrical current, electrical voltage of a magnetic field or a chemical reaction. "Smart Buildings" are buildings that make typological use of these new technologies.

"An apple-tree is the best sunshade", the great Austrian architect and urban planner Roland Rainer once lectured, not only calling for an ecological, user-friendly mode of construction in the 1950s, particularly in housing, but actually putting this principle into practice himself. "Smart Nature" for us is not about borrowing structures, techniques or forms from nature, for instance in Biomorphic Architecture, but rather using nature directly (e.g. plants, gases, liquids, etc.) as "Smart Materials" and "Smart Technologies". In this sense, "Smart Nature" means using organic or inorganic resources as building materials or combining them with each other or with artificially developed "Smart Technologies". Modern building typologies with façades incorporating bioreactors, in which algae are cultivated to generate energy and also to control light and shade of the entire building, can offer us an innovative system in the spirit of "Smart Nature" (↑ Fig. P. 18).

For an entry in the "Smart Material House" competition, SPLITTERWERK joined forces with Arup and Bollinger + Grohmann to put together an outstanding team dedicated to "intelligent building". Arup was responsible for consulting on "New Materials" and "Building Services" and Bollinger + Grohmann for the load-bearing structure. Together with the expert consultants from IMMOSOLAR and SSC, Bern's University of Applied Science – Architecture, Wood and Building, G.tecz, inHaus, with the collaboration of BASF, Bayer Material Science, Fielitz, Fraunhofer ISC, Glas Trösch, Dresden University of Technology – Institute for Building Construction, and OKALUX, and supervised by SPLITTERWERK the cooperation was brought to a successful conclusion, winning the competition in spring 2010. Hamburg's citizenship was highly enthusiastic about the "Smart Treefrog"! The idea of realising a building that makes use of algae photosynthesis to reduce CO_2 while also generating energy by utilising biomass and solar thermal power was a firm fixture in the media and politics of the Hanseatic city soon after its publication. After more than a year of the IBA looking for investors and a site, the local building developer and investor Otto Wulff showed an interest in developing and building a world-first building with the world's first algae photobioreactor facade together with us and our team for the IBA. The planning race against time began in summer 2011 – after all, the opening date of the IBA was set for spring 2013. In the end, we were able to meet this deadline. Since then, we have been carrying out extensive monitoring and research work on location. This prototypical multi-storey residential building on the IBA site in Hamburg Wilhelmsburg has meanwhile gained international fame as »BIQ« (Bio-Intelligence Quotient), "The Algae House" or "The Clever Treefrog".

Our sincere and heartfelt thanks are due to all those who enabled, encouraged and accompanied the participation of our SPLITTERWERK studio at the International Building Exhibition (IBA) Hamburg and, in this context, also to our interdisciplinary team consisting of professionals from a wide range of disciplines of science, research and practice. Successful realisation of the prototypical "Algae

wie die der Pflanzen und Tiere. Die Gebäudehaut beeinflusst z.B. de Energiehaushalt, die Blickbeziehungen (mögliche Aus- und Einblick(und das Erscheinungsbild eines Gebäudes wesentlich. Da die Haut d Nahtstelle zwischen dem einen und dem anderen Raum ist (z.B. Inne und Außenraum) macht es Sinn sehr viele funktionale Anforderunge in ihr aufzunehmen: Sie kann u.a. Licht absorbierend, reflektierend, u durchsichtig, transluzent, transparent, photovoltaisch, dämmend, sp(chernd, selbstleuchtend, vielfarbig, steuerbar, passiv, aktiv, interakt und reversibel sein. „Smart Skins" sind heutzutage meistens noch ei vielschichtige Kombination aus verschiedenen Bauelementen unte schiedlichster Materialien (dicke Wand), die in bestimmten Verhältni sen zueinander abwechselnd, je nach Anforderungen, die Gebäudehül bilden. Dabei werden neben tragenden, raumbildenden und bauphys kalisch wirksamen Materialien bzw. Materialkombinationen auch o tisch wirksame eingesetzt. Während „Smart Technologies" (intel gente Technologien) wie computergesteuerte Oberflächen aus LED un OLED rein optisch wirksam sind, können Farb- und Form- bzw. Gestal veränderungen bei „Smart Materials" reversibel durch Licht, Temp ratur, elektrischen Strom, elektrische Spannung eines Magnetfelde oder einer chemischen Reaktion erzielt werden. „Smart Building sind Gebäude, die sich diese neuen Technologien typologisch zunutz machen.

„Der Apfelbaum ist der beste Sonnenschutz", dozierte einst der groß österreichische Architekt und Städtebauer Roland Rainer, der scho in den 50er-Jahren des vergangenen Jahrhunderts für eine ökologisch und menschengerechte Bauweise besonders auch im Wohnbau nich nur plädierte, sondern diese auch umsetzte. Unter „Smart Nature" (i telligente Natur) verstehen wir nicht die strukturelle, technische ode formale Anleihe bei der Natur wie etwa in der biomorphen Architektu sondern die direkte Verwendung von Natur (wie Pflanzen, Gase, Flü sigkeiten u. dgl.) als „Smart Materials" bzw. „Smart Technologies „Smart Nature" bedeutet demnach den Einsatz von organischen ode anorganischen Ressourcen als Baumaterialien oder diese in Kombin tion miteinander bzw. in Kombination mit künstlich entwickelten „Sma Technologies". Zeitgemäße Gebäudetypen mit aus Bioreaktoren beste enden Fassaden, in denen Algen einerseits zur Energiegewinnung, and rerseits zur Lichtsteuerung und Beschattung des gesamten Gebäude gezüchtet werden, können uns ein neuartiges und innovatives Syster im Sinne von „Smart Nature" bereitstellen (↑ Abb. S. 18).

Für den Wettbewerb „Smart Material House" stellte SPLITTERWER mit Arup und mit Bollinger + Grohmann ein für die Thematik „intel gentes Bauen" hervorragendes Team zusammen. Arup war für da Consulting in den Bereichen „Neue Materialien" und „Haustechnol gie" verantwortlich und Bollinger + Grohmann für die Tragkonstruk on. Gemeinsam mit den Fachberatern von IMMOSOLAR und SSC, de Berner Fachhochschule – Architektur, Holz und Bau, G.tecz, inHau und in partnerschaftlicher Zusammenarbeit mit BASF, Bayer Materi Science, Fielitz, Fraunhofer ISC, Glas Trösch, Technische Universitä Dresden – Institut für Baukonstruktion und OKALUX konnte unter de Leitung von SPLITTERWERK die Zusammenarbeit im Frühjahr 2010 e folgreich mit dem Wettbewerbsgewinn abgeschlossen werden. Die Han burger Bürgerschaft war vom „Smart Treefrog" hellauf begeistert! Di Idee, ein Gebäude realisieren zu können, das sich die Photosynthese vo Algen zur CO_2-Reduktion bei gleichzeitiger Energiegewinnung durc Biomasseverwertung und Solarthermie zunutze macht, war bald nac ihrer Veröffentlichung aus Medien und Politik der Hansestadt nich mehr wegzudenken. Nach mehr als einjähriger Investoren- und Grund stückssuche der IBA zeigte der ortsansässige Bauunternehmer und I vestor Otto Wulff Interesse ein welterstes Gebäude mit der welterste Algenphotobioreaktorenfassade mit uns und unserem Team im Rahme der IBA entwickeln und realisieren zu wollen. Ab Sommer 2011 began dann der Planungswettlauf gegen die Zeit – schließlich war die Eröf nung der IBA mit Frühjahr 2013 fixiert. Der Zeitplan konnte letztend lich eingehalten werden. Seither werden vor Ort umfassende Monito ring- und Forschungsarbeiten durchgeführt. Dieser prototypische G schosswohnungsbau am IBA-Gelände in Hamburg Wilhelmsburg is mittlerweile unter den Bezeichnungen „BIQ" (für Bio-Intelligenz-Qu tient), „Das Algenhaus" oder auch „The Clever Treefrog" weltwe bekannt.

ouse" building project was only possible thanks to this unique am spirit. In connection with this, it is particularly important to us o draw your attention to the list of project authors of the book P. 4). We would also like to thank everyone involved in the book roject. Without their great commitment and support it would not ave been possible to carry out the project in such a short time. hanks, first and foremost, to Andrea Wiegelmann from niggli pub shers, who assisted our publication project from the outset, push ng us ahead in terms of content, design and timing with her expe ence and constantly positive criticism. Thank you to our partners om the public sector and business for the generous financial sup ort and/or for the numerous, friendly words of welcome and en ouraging congratulations at the start of the book. Thanks to Rudi cheuermann and Jan Wurm, both from Arup, not only for the cir umspect foreword, the absolutely lucid text about highly complex ngineering technology, and the important visuals, but above all, f course, for the excellent cooperation since 2009 and their enthu iasm for visionary ideas. Their personal commitment and the inter ational network of Arup was significantly involved in the success ul realisation of the building and book project. What would an archi ectural publication be without photos? Paul Ott has been photo raphing SPLITTERWERK's works since 1996, creating irretrievably aluable contemporary documents with his pictures. Warmest hanks for accompanying us over such a long time, for the collabo ation in Hamburg over a period of several days, and for the photo ssay. More than five years of project history results in a mountain f material that not only needs to be editorially inspected, ordered nd condensed. The ultimate aim is also to communicate this mate ial in an adequate manner in a publication. For this undertaking it vent without saying for us to win over the renowned Institute for ook Design and Media Development (Institut für Buchgestaltung nd Medienentwicklung) headed by Uli Cluss at the Stuttgart State cademy of Visual Arts (Staatliche Akademie der Bildenden Künste tuttgart). Nicolas Zupfer is responsible for the wonderful book esign. In hectic, difficult stages of the book project, he always ound optimistic words, radiating the necessary calm, and keeping is patience with us and the authors right up the last minute. Our reat thanks are therefore due to the "Book Institute" and particu larly to communication designer Nicolas Zupfer.

RUDI SCHEUERMANN
■ PREFACE

■ DIRECTOR ARUP DEUTSCHLAND GMBH
GLOBAL FAÇADE LEADER

■ In 2008 Peter Head, ex-Director of our firm and leader of our lobal planning practice, delivered his influential "Brunel Interna ional Lecture" at the Institution of Civil Engineers in London. He resented his model of the "ecological age", an approach towards new green vision for the planning and service infrastructure which ncluded façade-applied microalgae systems as a key element. Mi roalgae perform photosynthesis up to 10 times faster than higher lants, which allows the implementation of short carbon cycles and fficiently captures CO_2 emissions. This idea was adopted by the K Institution of Mechanical Engineers, and some architects had tarted to show algae systems in visual renderings. These first con epts, however, were all based on glass tubular bioreactors, in which vater and algae circulate through a meandering transparent tube to bsorb light and carbon – a costly and maintenance-intensive type of system, and not supported by a holistic building concept. n 2009, Arup established its Materials Consulting practice in main and Europe, and shortly afterwards the new consultancy was ap roached by the Austrian architectural practice SPLITTERWERK to join ts design team for a competition on a "Smart Material House for he International Building Exhibition (IBA), to take place in Hamburg n 2013. This competition proved to be the perfect occasion to com ine and develop the previous experience in this field of both firms.

Unser aufrichtiger und herzlicher Dank gilt all denen, die die Beteili gung unseres Ateliers SPLITTERWERK an der Internationalen Bauaus stellung (IBA) Hamburg ermöglicht, gefördert und begleitet haben, und in diesem Zusammenhang auch unserem interdisziplinären Team, bestehend aus den unterschiedlichsten Professionen in Wissenschaft, Forschung und Praxis. Erst durch diesen einzigartigen Teamgeist war eine erfolgreiche Realisierung des prototypischen Bauprojekts „Algen haus" überhaupt möglich. In diesem Zusammenhang ist es uns ganz besonders wichtig, auf die Nennung der Projektverfasser im Buch zu verweisen (↑ S. 4). Weiters bedanken wir uns herzlich bei allen Mit wirkenden des Buchprojekts, ohne deren großes Engagement und Unterstützung die Realisierung innerhalb einer so kurzen Zeit nicht möglich gewesen wäre. Allen voran gilt hier der Dank Andrea Wiegel mann vom niggli Verlag, die unser Publikationsvorhaben von Anbe ginn an unterstützte und uns mit ihrer Erfahrung und immer positiven Kritik inhaltlich, gestalterisch und zeitlich vorantrieb. Unseren Part nern aus öffentlicher Hand und Wirtschaft danken wir für die groß zügige finanzielle Unterstützung und/oder für die zahlreichen, freund lichen Grußworte und ermunternden Glückwünsche am Buchanfang. Rudi Scheuermann und Jan Wurm, beide von Arup, danken wir nicht nur für das umsichtige Vorwort, den bestens verständlichen Text über komplexeste Ingenieurtechnologie und die wichtigen Abbildungsbei träge, sondern vor allem natürlich auch für die großartige Zusammen arbeit seit 2009 und ihre Begeisterung für visionäre Ideen. Ihr persön licher Einsatz und das internationale Netzwerk von Arup waren maß geblich beteiligt bei der erfolgreichen Realisierung des Bau- und Buch projekts. Was wäre eine Architekturpublikation ohne Fotos? Paul Ott fotografiert seit 1996 die Arbeiten von SPLITTERWERK und schafft mit seinen Lichtbildern für uns unwiederbringlich wertvolle Zeitdoku mente. Für die Begleitung über einen so langen Zeitraum, die tage lange Zusammenarbeit in Hamburg und den Fotoessay ganz, ganz lie ben Dank. Mehr als fünf Jahre Projektgeschichte ergibt einen haus hohen Stapel an Material, der nicht nur redaktionell gesichtet, geord net und verdichtet werden muss, sondern letztendlich auch in einer Publikation adäquat kommuniziert werden soll. Für uns lag es natür lich sofort auf der Hand dazu das renommierte Institut für Buchgestal tung und Medienentwicklung unter der Leitung von Uli Cluss an der Staatlichen Akademie der Bildenden Künste Stuttgart gewinnen zu wollen. Für die wunderbare Gestaltung des Buches ist Nicolas Zupfer verantwortlich. Er hat auch in hektischen und schwierigen Phasen des Publikationsprojekts immer optimistische Worte gefunden, die notwendige Ruhe weitergegeben und seine Geduld mit uns und den Autoren bis zur letzten Sekunde bewahrt. Nicht zuletzt gilt also unser großer Dank dem „Buchinstitut" und im Besonderen dem Kommuni kationsdesigner Nicolas Zupfer.

RUDI SCHEUERMANN
□ VORWORT

□ DIREKTOR ARUP DEUTSCHLAND GMBH
LEITER GLOBAL FAÇADE

□ Im Jahr 2008 hielt Peter Head, ehemaliger Direktor unseres Unternehmens und Leiter unserer internationalen Planungsabtei lung die weithin Impulse gebende „Brunel International Lecture" (Brunel International Lesung) in der Institution of Civil Engineers (Berufsverband der Bauingenieure) in London. Er stellte sein Mo dell des „Ökologischen Zeitalters" vor, eine Annäherung an eine neue grüne Vision von Planung und Infrastruktur, zu der Mikroalgen Fassadensysteme als Schlüsselelement zählten. Die Photosynthese von Mikroalgen erfolgt zehnmal schneller als bei höheren Pflanzen, was die Kohlenstoffzyklen verkürzt und CO_2-Emissionen effizient absorbiert. Die Institution of Mechanical Engineers (Berufsverband der Gebäudetechnik) des Vereinigten Königreichs nahm sich des Vor schlags an, und einige Architekten begannen, in ihren Visualisierun gen Algensysteme darzustellen. Diese ersten Konzepte basierten je doch auf Bioreaktoren aus Glasröhren, in denen Wasser und Algen durch ein mäanderndes transparentes Rohr zirkulieren, um Licht und

Working on the "Supernature" skin of the scheme, the Arup competition support team led by Jan Wurm identified a small hydrobiology specialist company called Strategic Science Consult GmbH (SSC) in Hamburg, which was researching processes for cultivating microalgae. On an open field test site SSC had developed and tested a flat panel bioreactor that could turn daylight into biomass with an efficiency of close to 10%. This was achieved through air uplift technology, where pressurized air is injected at the bottom of the panel and the turbulences created by rising air bubbles stimulate the absorption of carbon and light. Our team then developed the first sketches showing the implementation of flat panel bioreactors on the building skin and integration in the energy concept of the "Smart Material House". It is a great tribute to the spirit of collaboration between individuals in other constituents of the "Smart Material House" design team, namely Mark Blaschitz of SPLITTERWERK, Karsten Peleikis at the time working for IMMOSOLAR GmbH and Martin Kerner of SSC, that this initial concept of a bio-responsive façade for the external skin was adopted and developed further.

In March 2010 the IBA announced that the project had won a first prize. The bio-responsive façade was highlighted by the jury as the key component of innovation. Our office in Berlin was instrumental in pulling together an industry consortium for developing and testing the system that currently also involves Colt International, a global player in façade and climate engineering components. Thanks to the commitment of Lukas Verlage, Ulrich Kremer, Manfred Starlinger and Jörg Ribbecke of the Colt team, a façade system for the building integration was able to be jointly developed in a time frame of only just over two years. The project received substantial funding from "Zukunft Bau" (future building) initiative of the German Federal Ministry of Transport, Building and Urban Development (Bundesministerium für Verkehr, Bau und Stadtentwicklung (BMVBS) and the support of Ministerialrat Hans-Dieter Hegner and Guido Hagel from the Federal Institute for Research on Building, Urban Affairs and Spatial Development (Bundesinstitut für Bau-, Stadt- und Raumforschung (BBSR) in securing the funding was essential. It is at this point that the ownership structure of Arup as an organization made a big difference to the success of the project. As a trust, our company belongs to our staff and is not controlled by short-term objectives of external shareholders. Every year we re-invest about a third of our profit in research activities and external collaborations to help shape a better built environment. Although this technology did not hold a promise for a quick return of investment, the firm committed to match-fund its development. In order to deliver best practice, we involved our key specialists around the globe in the field of Materials Science, Glass Design, Energy Simulations, Façade Engineering, Building Physics, MEP Design and Information Communication Technology (ICT), bringing a truly inter-disciplinary team of experts together.

We are tremendously grateful that we have been able to help make this project a success. The "BIQ-House" demonstrates our culture of innovation and creativity, our independence and commitment to research, the unique breadth and depth of our skills and specially the belief that the current and future challenges can only be solved by close and trusted collaborations.

Kohlenstoff zu absorbieren – ein teures System mit aufwändiger Instandhaltung ohne Gesamtbaukonzept.

Im Jahr 2009 begründete Arup den Kompetenzbereich Materials Consulting auf dem Kontinent. Kurz darauf trat das österreichische Architekturbüro SPLITTERWERK an Arup heran, um gemeinsam ein „Smart Material House" für einen Wettbewerb anlässlich der Internationalen Bauausstellung in Hamburg 2013 zu entwerfen. Dieser Wettbewerb bot die perfekte Gelegenheit, die bisherige einschlägige Erfahrung beider Büros miteinander zu verbinden und weiterzuentwickeln.

Das Arup-Team unter der Leitung von Jan Wurm arbeitete an der „Supernature"-Hülle des Projekts. In diesem Zusammenhang wandte es sich an eine kleine auf Hydrobiologie spezialisierte Firma namens Strategic Science Consult GmbH (SSC) in Hamburg, die im Bereich Mikroalgenzuchtprozesse Forschung betreibt. In einem offenen Feldversuch hatte SSC einen Flachpaneel-Bioreaktor entwickelt, der Tageslicht mit einem Wirkungsgrad von beinahe zehn Prozent in Biomasseverwandelte. Erzielt wurde dieser Wert durch eine Luftwirbeltechnik, bei der Pressluft auf den Boden des Paneels eingeblasen wird; die durch aufsteigende Luftblasen erzeugten Turbulenzen fördern die Absorption von Kohlenstoff und Licht. Unser Team entwickelte dann die ersten Skizzen, auf denen man den Einbau flacher Bioreaktor-Paneele in die Außenhaut und die Integration des Energiekonzepts des „Smart Material House" sieht. Dank des Teamgeistes aller Mitglieder im „Smart Material House"-Entwurfsteam, insbesondere Mark Blaschitz von SPLITTERWERK, Karsten Peleikis, der zu dieser Zeit für die IMMOSOLAR GmbH arbeitete, sowie Martin Kerner von SSC, konnte das ursprüngliche Konzept einer bioadaptiven Fassade für die Außenhaut angenommen und weiterentwickelt werden.

Im März 2010 gab die Internationale Bauausstellung IBA bekannt, dass der Entwurf den ersten Preis gewonnen hatte. Dabei wurde die bioadaptive Fassade von der Jury als innovative Schlüsselkomponente gewertet. Unser Berliner Büro war wesentlich an der Zusammenstellung einer Industrie-ARGE für die Entwicklung und den Test des Systems beteiligt, an der auch Colt International, ein Global Player im Bereich von Komponenten für Fassaden- und Klimaverfahrenstechnik, beteiligt ist. Dank des Engagements von Lukas Verlage, Ulrich Kremer, Manfred Starlinger und Jörg Ribbecke vom Colt-Team konnte in gerade mal gut zwei Jahren ein Fassadensystem bis zur Baureife entwickelt werden. Das Projekt wurde von der Initiative „Zukunft Bau" des Bundesministeriums für Verkehr, Bau und Stadtentwicklung (BMVBS) mitfinanziert und von Ministerialrat Hans-Dieter Hegner und Guido Hagel vom Bundesinstitut für Bau Stadt- und Raumforschung (BBSR) begleitet.

Für den Erfolg des Projekts war auch die Eigentümerstruktur von Arup entscheidend. Als Stiftung gehört unsere Firma unseren Mitarbeitern und wird nicht von kurzfristigen Erfolgszielen externer Aktionäre gesteuert. Jedes Jahr reinvestieren wir ungefähr ein Drittel unseres Gewinns in Forschungsaktivitäten und externe Kooperationen, um einen Beitrag zur besseren Gestaltung der gebauten Umwelt zu leisten. Obwohl diese Technologie keine schnelle Rendite versprach, beschloss das Büro die Entwicklung mitzufinanzieren. Um „Best Practice" liefern zu können, banden wir unsere Experten aus den Bereichen Material Science, Glasdesign, Energiesimulation, Fassaden-Engineering, Bauphysik, Haustechnik und Informations und Kommunikationstechnologie ein, was ein effizientes interdisziplinäres Expertenteam ergab.

Wir sind hocherfreut, dass es uns gelungen ist, diesem Projekt zum Erfolg zu verhelfen. Das „BIQ-Haus" ist ein weiterer Beweis für unsere Innovationskraft und Kreativität, die auf unserer Unabhängigkeit und Neugierde beruhen. Sie zeigt die Bandbreite unserer Kompetenzen und bestätigt unsere Überzeugung, dass aktuelle und künftige Herausforderungen nur durch eine enge und vertrauensvolle Zusammenarbeit gemeistert werden können.

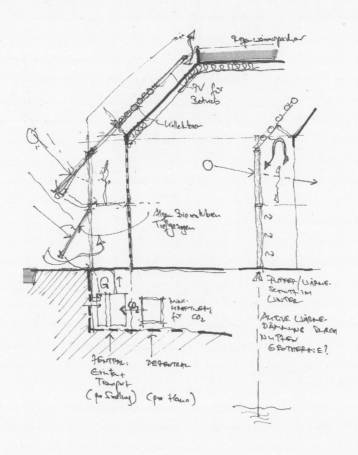

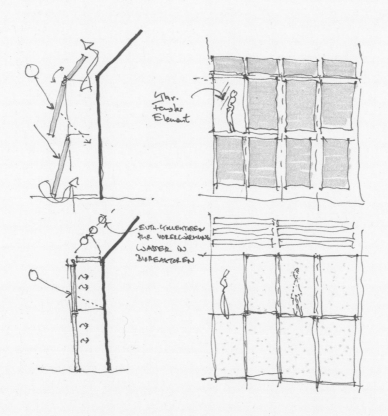

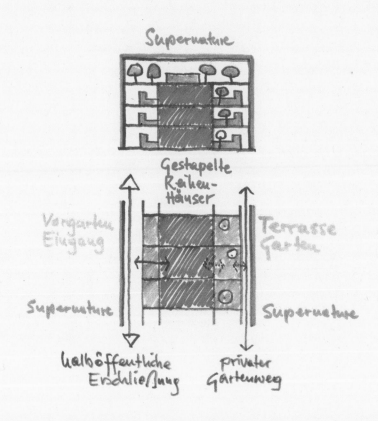

Supernature

Gestapelte
Reihen-
Häuser

Vorgarten
Eingang

Terrasse
Garten

Supernature

Supernature

halböffentliche
Erschließung

privater
Gartenweg

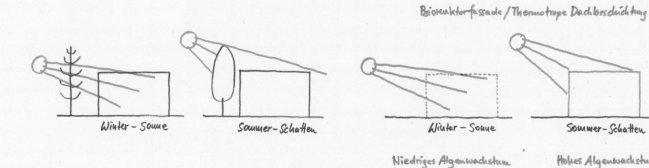

Bioreaktorfassade / Thermotrope Dachbeschichtung

Winter - Sonne

Sommer-Schatten

Winter - Sonne

Sommer-Schatten

Niedriges Algenwachstum

Hohes Algenwachstum

SPLITTERWERK ■ BIQ / THE ALGAE HOUSE / THE CLEVER TREEFROG

This visionary "Case Study House" featuring the first algae bioreactor façade world-wide was realised in the frame of the International Building Exhibition (IBA) in Hamburg in 2012 and 2013. As "Smart Material House", it combines smart materials and technologies with smart typologies of living.

ARCHITECTURAL MASTERPIECE

Setting the scene with its two red-white-red-white striped sunny-sided algae bioreactor façades, this janiform structure is reminiscent of the colours associated with the Free and Hanseatic city of Hamburg, or if you like, with the Alpine Republic of Austria – but above all – they emphasize the uniqueness of this multi-storey residential building and its prototypical method of producing energy and regulating light and sun-shading (↑ Fig. p. 6–7). At close range, the façades – oscillating from afar through the constantly growing algae – start to move; bubbles forming through the supply of carbon dioxide and nitrogen, as well as the permanently essential circulation of water containing aerosol-like micro-algae, seem to suggest that biomass production could be a solar-powered art installation, steadily bubbling along (↑ Fig. p. 55–59). From afar, you can already read two giant speech bubbles with black letters against a white background shown on the two green shady façades with their tiny windows, the first bubble asking "Photosynthesis?" and the second replying "Cool!" (↑ Fig. p. 48). "Realisation also means communication", SPLITTERWERK engineers, architects and artists assert and let the top of two penthouse façades entwine with grape-vine ornaments (↑ Fig. p. 50, 51).

ENERGY HYBRID

Thanks to the hybrid functionality of its algae façade, it is possible to combine various processes of regenerative energy production to create a sustainable circulation system in this building: solar heat, geothermal energy as well as biomass production and exploitation (e.g. as biogas by means of a fuel cell). Biogas is the result of a natural process, i.e. of the microbial decomposition of organic matter under anoxic conditions. Microorganisms then transform carbohydrates, proteins and fats – contained in the microalgae – into methane and carbon dioxide, which requires anoxic conditions, i.e. the absence of oxygen. Moreover, the façade can fulfil all functions expected of a conventional building cladding: it not only acts as a thermal and sound insulation, but also as a sun shield.

129 translucent, plate-shaped glass containers – so-called photo bioreactors – are composed of two structurally bonded glass panes, the outer structural glass pane having been manufactured as a photovoltaic module glass. In the container itself, microalgae are cultivated in a watery culture medium that then perform photosynthesis by absorbing natural light, subsequently also producing biomass when supplied with carbon dioxide and the nutrients nitrogen and phosphor (↑ Fig. p. 58–62). They are able to store carbon dioxide and produce biogas that is transformed in the in-house fuel cell, which generates 4,500 KWH per year. Moreover, the photo bioreactors' solar thermal function additionally produces around 32 MW heat per year that can either be directly used in the house or fed into the local power network, or alternatively, temporarily stored underground.

RESIDENTIAL TYPOLOGY

Whether it be Mies van der Rohe's flowing space, Frank Lloyd Wright's open floor plan, or Adolf Loos's "Raumplan", not to

---

SPLITTERWERK □ BIQ / DAS ALGENHAUS / THE CLEVER TREEFROG

□ Das zukunftsweisende „Case Study House" mit der weltweit ersten Algenbioreaktorfassade wurde im Rahmen der Internationalen Bauausstellung (IBA) Hamburg in den Jahren 2012 und 2013 realisiert. Dieses „Smart Material House" vereint intelligente Materialien und Technologien mit intelligenten Typologien des Wohnens.

BAUKUNSTWERK

Der janusköpfige Baukörper inszeniert seine beiden sonnseitigen Algenbioreaktorfassaden mit rot-weiß-rot-weißen Streifen und erinnert so vielleicht an die Farben der Hansestadt, wer will, auch an die der Alpenrepublik, vor allem aber wird die Einzigartigkeit des Geschosswohnbaus und sein prototypischer Betrieb von Photobioreaktoren zur Energieerzeugung, Lichtsteuerung und Beschattung unterstrichen (↑ Abb. S. 6–7). Einmal nähergekommen, geraten die von der Ferne durch das stetige Wachstum der Algen farblich changierenden Fassaden in Bewegung: Blasenbildung durch Kohlenstoffdioxid- und Stickstoffzufuhr und die stetig notwendige Zirkulation des Wassers mit den schwebstoffartig erscheinenden Mikroalgen legen einem die Interpretation nahe, die Biomasseerzeugung sei in Wirklichkeit eine solar betriebene Kunstinstallation, die leise vor sich hin blubbert (↑ Abb. S. 55–59). Schattenseitig ist schon von Weitem auf zwei grünen Fassaden mit winzigen Fenstern in riesigen Sprechblasen mit schwarzer Schrift auf weißem Grund die Frage „Photosynthese?" mit der darauf gleich folgenden Antwort „Cool!" zu lesen (↑ Abb. S. 48). „Realisieren bedeutet auch kommunizieren", behaupten dazu die Ingenieure, Architekten und Künstler von SPLITTERWERK und lassen zu guter Letzt und ganz oben an zwei Penthausfassaden Weinreben aus Ornamentputz ranken (↑ Abb. S. 50–51).

ENERGIEHYBRID

Dank der hybriden Funktionalität der Algenfassade ist es möglich, im Gebäude verschiedene Prozesse regenerativer Energiegewinnung zu einem nachhaltigen Kreislaufsystem zu vereinen: Solarthermie, Geothermie, und Biomasseproduktion und -verwertung (z.B. als Biogas mittels einer Brennstoffzelle). Biogas entsteht durch den natürlichen Prozess des mikrobiellen Abbaus organischer Stoffe unter anoxischen Bedingungen. Dabei setzen Mikroorganismen die in den Mikroalgen enthaltenen Kohlenhydrate, Eiweiße und Fette in die Hauptprodukte Methan und Kohlenstoffdioxid um. Dafür sind anoxische Verhältnisse notwendig, also die Abwesenheit von Sauerstoff. Darüber hinaus kann die Fassade alle Funktionen eines konventionellen Gebäudekleids erfüllen. Sie dient sowohl der Wärme- und Kälteisolation als auch dem Schall- und Sonnenschutz.

Die 129 lichtdurchlässigen, plattenförmigen Glascontainer, die sogenannten Photobioreaktoren, werden aus je zwei strukturell miteinander verklebten Glasscheiben gebildet, wobei die äußere Strukturglasscheibe als „Photovoltaik-Modul-Glas" ausgeführt wurde. Im Inneren der Container werden in einem wässrigen Kulturmedium Mikroalgen kultiviert, die unter Sonneneinstrahlung und Zufuhr von Kohlenstoffdioxid und den Nährstoffen Stickstoff und Phosphor Photosynthese betreiben und damit Biomasse produzieren (↑ Abb. S. 58–62). Über diese wird sowohl Kohlenstoffdioxid gespeichert als auch Biogas gewonnen, das in einer hausinternen Brennstoffzelle in rund 4.500 Kilowattstunden pro Jahr umgewandelt werden soll. Darüber hinaus kann die solarthermische Funktion der Photobioreaktoren zusätzlich rund 32 Megawatt Wärme pro Jahr erzeugen,

mention Margarete Schütte-Lihotzky's economical Frankfurt Kitchen – their contemporary development is incorporated in the intelligent residential typologies of the "Case Study House" Clever Treefrog. In the adjustable structure of these new residential typologies, functional spaces can be alternately or simultaneously attached or detached on demand. The Loos plan thus becomes an individual and time-oriented living plan. The appearance of living space is dominated by user-oriented living requirements and changes of programme. Accordingly, "Smart Spaces" develop in the "Hamburg apartment" (↑ Fig. p. 65–76) and "Milan apartment" (↑ Fig. p. 85–89) from different typologies of reconfigurable floor plans.

RECONCEPTION

The "Incidents – We Love It!" series, on which SPLITTERWERK have been working since 2012, are at the same time pursuing strategies of reconception, assertion and appropriation. By using different classifications for "incidents" (German: Vorfälle, Ereignisse, Fehler, amongst others) found in their architecture, SPLITTERWERK claim them as works of art, at the same time confirming their authorship by means of naming and labelling the works. With this reinterpretation and appropriation, SPLITTERWERK reunite international architectural developments which are increasingly drifting apart in terms of conception, design, detailed design and realisation. The "BIQ – the Algae House – the Clever Treefrog" project presented at the International Building Exhibition in Hamburg was able to realise the three works "The Hamburg Apartment Incident" (↑ Fig. p. 80–81, 90–91), "The Milan Apartment Incident" and "The Speech Bubble Incident".

DREAM OF FLYING

Icarus and Daedalus, Leonardo da Vinci, Gustave Trouvé, Albrecht Ludwig Berblinger, Otto Lilienthal, the Wright Brothers, and many others with their airships and flying machines were all pioneers of aeronautics. They researched, constructed and experimented, were initially successful and sometimes failed. What they all had in common was their dream of flying and their tireless spirit of research for a constantly changing world. Today, we do not know as yet whether our "algae house" will ultimately be purposeful or if bioreactor technology will prove to be forward-looking, architecturally suitable, ecologically and economically worthwhile, dispensable or even be classified as dangerous. Nevertheless, SPLITTERWERK has always been convinced that it is also important and necessary again and again to translate one's visions into practice, no matter how unattainable they may seem at first.

JAN WURM
■ SOLAR LEAF – THE BIO-RESPONSIVE FAÇADE

■ ASSOCIATE DIRECTOR / MATERIALS CONSULTING ARUP GERMANY

■ Bioenergy accounts for over 8% of Germany's entire energy consumption. Biomass is the second largest source of renewable energy after wind power with regard to the production of electricity. One of its major advantages is that it is available as a solid (e.g. wood pellets), fluid (e.g. biodiesel), or as biogas, thus making it extremely versatile for use in electricity and heat production. Unlike electrical power from photovoltaics or wind energy, biomass is a form of solar energy that can be stored without any substantial losses and which does not require cost-intensive energy storage technology such as batteries. Basically, the conversion of biomass into energy is CO_2 neutral, because the quantity of carbon dioxide emitted through combustion is exactly the same as the quantity absorbed through photosynthesis from the atmosphere during plant growth.

die direkt im Haus genutzt oder in das Nahwärmenetz eingespei beziehungsweise im Erdboden zwischengespeichert wird.

WOHNTYPOLOGIE

Der fließende Raum von Mies van der Rohe oder der offene Grundri von Frank Lloyd Wright, der Raumplan von Adolf Loos, aber auch d Ökonomie der Frankfurter Küche von Margarete Schütte-Lihotzky fi den ihre zeitgemäße Weiterentwicklung in den intelligenten Wohntyp logien des „Case Study House" Clever Treefrog. Im schaltbaren G füge dieser neuen Wohnungstypologien werden Funktionsräume wec selnd oder gleichzeitig – on demand – zu und wieder weggeschalte Der Loos'sche Raumplan wird zum individuellen und verzeitlichte Wohnplan. Der zeitliche Wohnablauf, das wechselnde Programm, prä(userorientiert das Erscheinungsbild der Wohnung. So entstehen in d „Hamburger Wohnung" (↑ Abb. S. 65–76) und der „Mailänder Wo nung" (↑ Abb. S. 85–89) „Smart Spaces" mit unterschiedlichen Typ logien re-konfigurierbarer Grundrisse.

RE-KONZEPTION

Die Serien „Incidents – We Love It!", an der SPLITTERWERK se 2012 arbeiten, verfolgen gleichzeitig Strategien der Re-konzeptio Behauptung und Aneignung. SPLITTERWERK erheben mittels unte schiedlicher Kennzeichnungen an ihren Architekturen vorgefund ne „incidents" (auf Deutsch u.a. Vorfälle, Ereignisse, Fehler) z Kunstwerken und behaupten gleichzeitig mittels einer Werksbene nung und -beschilderung ihre Autorenschaft. SPLITTERWERK führe mit dieser nachträglichen Interpretation und Aneignung die mit d Internationalisierung des Baugeschehens voranschreitende Tre nung zwischen Konzeption, Entwurf, Ausführungsplanung un Realisation wieder zusammen. Im Projekt „BIQ – Das Algenhaus The Clever Treefrog" auf der Internationalen Bauausstellung Har burg konnten die drei Arbeiten „The Hamburg Apartment Inciden „The Milan Apartment Incident" (↑ Abb. S. 80–81, 90–91) und „Th Speech Bubble Incident" realisiert werden.

TRAUM VOM FLIEGEN

Ikaros und Daidalos, Leonardo da Vinci, Gustave Trouvé, Albrec Ludwig Berblinger, Otto Lilienthal, die Gebrüder Wright und viel andere mehr waren mit ihren Luftschiffen und Flugmaschinen all samt Pioniere der Aeronautik. Sie recherchierten, konstruierten un experimentierten, hatten erste Erfolge und scheiterten mitunter. G mein ist ihnen allen aber ihr Traum vom Fliegen und ihr unermü licher Forschergeist für eine sich ständig verändernde Welt! W wissen heute noch nicht ob wir mit dem „Algenhaus" einen letz endlich zielführenden Weg vorzeigen können und ob die Bioreaktc technologie als zukunftsweisend, architekturtauglich, ökologisc und wirtschaftlich sinnvoll, entbehrlich oder gar als gefährlich ei gestuft werden muss. Jedenfalls war und ist SPLITTERWERK d von überzeugt, dass es immer wieder auch wichtig und notwendi ist Visionen – und erscheinen sie uns vorerst auch noch so fern in die Realität zu übersetzen.

JAN WURM
□ SOLAR LEAF – DIE BIO-ADAPTIVE FASSADE

■ ASSOCIATE DIRECTOR / MATERIALS CONSULTING ARUP DEUTSCHLAND

□ Mehr als acht Prozent des gesamten Energieverbrauchs Deutschland werden aus Bioenergie gedeckt. Bei der Stromerze gung ist Biomasse nach der Windkraft die zweitgrößte erneuerbar Energiequelle. Einer ihrer wesentlichen Vorteile ist, dass sie sowo in fester (z.B. Holzpellets) als auch in flüssiger Form (z.B. Biodiese oder als Biogas vorliegt und sich so auf ungemein vielfältige Weis zur Strom und Wärmeerzeugung nutzen lässt. Anders als Photov

oday, microalgae belong to the most promising factors in alterna-
ive energy scenarios, since they convert sunlight into biomass
specially effectively. Just like other plants, microalgae use sun-
ght for the photosynthetic process in which CO_2 is degraded. This
orks in the same way with higher plant species. However, micro-
lgae are much more efficient in converting light energy into bio-
nass than higher plants, because they are unicellular and each sin-
gle cell is involved in the process of photosynthesis.

s opposed to energy crops such as maize, cultivating microalgae
oes not require additional agricultural land that would compete
vith food production. Besides, since microalgae can be cultivated
n photobioreactors (PBR), they are neither dependent on weather
onditions, nor intensive farming methods. PBRS are closed, trans-
arent, hollow containers filled with a culture medium that can be
et up in places where it would be otherwise too dry or barren, thus
ideal for use in large cities.

he advantages of microalgae led to the development of the world's
rst photobioreactor façade based on these kinds of microorga-
isms. It was installed as a prototype in a multi-family house as part
f the International Building Exhibition (IBA) in Hamburg-Wilhelmsburg at the beginning of 2013.

GERMANY'S FIRST BIO-RESPONSIVE FAÇADE

n 2009, Austrian SPLITTERWERK architects invited the engineer-
ng firm Arup to join them in an architectural competition for a
Smart Material House" that was to be built for the IBA 2013 in
lamburg. The design featured a translucent envelope that would
nclose the multi-storey building like a "second skin", thus cre-
ting a thermal buffer zone. One of the concept's essential com-
onents was a façade-applied microalgae system that would
upply the building with energy generated from solar heat and
biomass.

uring the competition stage, our design team had already entered
nto a co-operation with Strategic Science Consult (SSC), a con-
ulting firm specialising in hydrobiology. In a field test, SSC tested
flat photobioreactor that converts sunlight into biomass with an
nergy conversion efficiency of 10%. This is achieved through air
plift technology in a façade panel filled with algae and water that
vorks in a similar way to established biomass conversion processes.
his method involves injecting pressurized air at the bottom of the
anel, while the turbulences created by rising air bubbles stimulate
he absorption of carbon and light through the algae. At the same
ime, the mixture of algae and water continually "washes" the
nner surfaces of the panel with its rapid movements – a process
hat can be seen with the naked eye. Moreover, the flat photobiore-
ctors are more efficient than tubular ones and only require minimal
maintenance.

ur scheme convinced the jury and in March 2010 the IBA announced
hat the team SPLITTERWERK, including Arup, had won a first prize.
he bio-responsive facade was praised as a key achievement in building innovation.

n the industrial consortium that had been initiated by Arup in the
ame year, SSC was responsible for the process technology, whi-
e façade specialist Colt International from Kleve took over the
ob of system and detail development as well as the procurement.
rup was responsible for concept development, engineering and
coordination.

his development work resulted in an external shading system con-
isting of floor-to-ceiling glass lamellas with integrated photobioreactors and solar thermal absorbers.

he louvers are supported on the vertical axis to track the path of
he sun. All services, such as the supply of pressurized air, inlet and
utlet of the watery algae solution are integrated in the perimeter
raming. The configuration of the glass units comprise four panes of
nonolithic glass forming a central cavity of 18 MM for the circula-
ion of the medium which can contain 24 litres of algae medium.
n either side of the bioreactor are insulating cavities. The front
lass pane is a laminated extra-clear safety glass featuring anti-
reflective rolled glass to maximise the solar gain.

taik oder Windstrom ist Biomasse eine Form der Solarenergie, die
sich praktisch verlustfrei speichern lässt und ohne die Verwendung
kostenträchtiger Speichertechnologien wie Batterien auskommt.
Die Umwandlung von Biomasse in Energie ist grundsätzlich CO_2-
neutral, denn die Menge des bei der Verbrennung ausgestoßenen
Kohlendioxids entspricht genau der Menge, die während des Pflan-
zenwachstums durch Photosynthese aus der Atmosphäre aufgenom-
men wurde.

Mikroalgen zählen heute zu den vielversprechenden Bausteinen al-
ternativer Energieszenarien, da sie Sonnenlicht besonders effektiv
in Biomasse umwandeln. Wie andere Pflanzen nutzen Mikroalgen
das Sonnenlicht für den photosynthetischen Prozess, bei dem CO_2
abgebaut wird. Dieser läuft in gleicher Weise bei höheren Pflanzen-
arten ab. Allerdings sind Mikroalgen wesentlich effizienter in der Umwandlung von Lichtenergie in Biomasse als höhere Pflanzen, weil sie
einzellig sind und jede dieser Zellen Photosynthese betreibt.

Im Gegensatz zum Anbau von Energiepflanzen wie Mais erfordert
die Zucht von Mikroalgen keine zusätzliche Landnahme, die in Kon-
kurrenz zur Kultivierung von Nahrungspflanzen stehen würde. Außer-
dem besteht keine Abhängigkeit von Witterungseinflüssen und intensiver Bewirtschaftung. Mikroalgen können in Photobioreaktoren
(PBR) kultiviert werden. PBR sind geschlossene, lichtdurchlässige
und mit einem Kulturmedium gefüllte Hohlkörper, die auch dort installiert werden können, wo es sonst zu trocken oder karg ist – also
auch mitten in der Großstadt.

Die Vorteile der Mikroalgen führten zur Entwicklung der weltweit
ersten Photobioreaktor-Fassade, die auf dieser Art Mikroorganismen basiert. Sie wurde Anfang 2013 als Prototyp in einem im Rahmen der Internationalen Bauausstellung (IBA) in Hamburg-Wilhelmsburg entstandenen Geschosswohnungsbau installiert.

DEUTSCHLANDS ERSTE BIO-ADAPTIVE FASSADE

Im Jahr 2009 luden die österreichischen Architekten SPLITTERWERK
das Ingenieurbüro Arup ein, sich mit ihnen am Architektenwettbe-
werb für ein „Smart Material House" zu beteiligen, das im Rahmen
der IBA 2013 in Hamburg errichtet werden sollte. Der Entwurf sah
eine durchscheinende Hüllkonstruktion vor, die den Geschosswohnungsbau als „zweite Haut" umschließen und auf diese Weise eine
thermische Pufferzone entstehen lassen sollte. Ein wesentlicher Be-
standteil des Konzepts war das fassadenintegrierte Mikroalgensys-
tem, das sowohl Solarwärme als auch Biomasse zur Energieversorgung des Gebäudes gewinnen sollte.

Bereits in der Wettbewerbsphase ging unser Entwurfsteam eine
Zusammenarbeit mit der auf Gewässerbiologie spezialisierten Bera-
tungsfirma Strategic Science Consult (SSC) ein. In einem Feldtest
entwickelte und testete SSC einen flachen Photobioreaktor, der Sonnenlicht mit einem Wirkungsgrad von zehn Prozent in Biomasse um-
wandelt. Erreicht wird dies durch eine aufwärtsgerichtete Luftströ-
mung in dem mit Algen und Wasser gefüllten Fassadenpaneel, wie
sie in ähnlicher Form auch bei bisherigen Prozessen der Biomasse-
verarbeitung verwendet wird. Dabei wird Luft mit Überdruck am
unteren Ende in das Paneel eingeleitet. Die durch die aufsteigenden
Luftblasen hervorgerufenen Turbulenzen stimulieren die CO_2- und
Lichtabsorption der Algen. Gleichzeitig „wäscht" das „Algen-Wasser-
Gemisch" durch seine schnelle Bewegung ständig die Innenober-
flächen des Paneels ab – ein Vorgang, der sich auch mit bloßem
Auge beobachten lässt. Die flachen Photobioreaktoren sind nicht
nur effizienter als solche in Röhrenform, sondern verursachen auch
nur einen minimalen Wartungsaufwand.

Unser Entwurfskonzept überzeugte die Jury, sodass das Team im
Jahr 2010 als einer der Sieger aus dem Wettbewerb hervorging.
Insbesondere die bio-adaptive Fassade wurde dabei als wesentliche
Innovation hervorgehoben. In dem von Arup im gleichen Jahr initi-
ierten Industriekonsortium zeichnete SSC für die Prozesstechno-
logie verantwortlich, während der Fassadenspezialist Colt International aus Kleve für die System- und Detailentwicklung sowie die
Beschaffung der Komponenten gewonnen wurde. Arup war für
die Konzeptentwicklung, das „Engineering" und die Koordinaten
verantwortlich.

THE WORLDWIDE FAÇADE'S DEBUT – THE "BIQ" IN HAMBURG

The four-storey residence »BIQ« in Hamburg comprises 129 elements of photobioreactors covering about 200M² net surface area. The algae façade was installed as a secondary structure in front of the southwest and southeast façade. Each façade element measures 2.5 M X 0.7 M; all panels of each storey are linked as a closed loop system with the plant room on the ground floor. The building's management centre monitors all the inlets and outlets of each cluster, their nutrient supply and the "algae harvest" at the interface with the building services system. Algae concentration and temperature of the solution are also checked at this interface. Heat generated through the solar thermal effect in the bioreactors needs to be dissipated in order to prevent the system from overheating. The temperature is kept below 40°C to ensure consistent energy production. A heat exchanger extracts excess heat from the system, which is either directly used for hot water supply – supported by a heat pump if necessary – or stored in the ground via geothermal probes. The algae biomass, an estimated 15G of dry mass per square metre façade and day, is either continually harvested or in batches. Harvesting is carried out through "flotation" in a cylindrical vessel, in which pressurized air fully automatically froths up and skims off the algae.

With the »BIQ« pilot project realised in Hamburg, the "biomass potential" corresponds to approx. 30KWH per square metre façade and year, and solar thermal heat gain amounts to around 150 KWH/M²A. The algae façade reduces the building's total CO_2 emission by about six tons per year; in addition, the biomass absorbs 2.5 tons of CO_2 from the flue gas supplied per year.

FURTHER DEVELOPMENTS AND OUTLOOK

Ever since the building project was launched in April 2013, Arup, SSC and Colt have carried out a comprehensive monitoring programme in co-operation with the HafenCity University, Hamburg, which has received substantial funding from the research initiative "Zukunft Bau" (Future Building). This involves monitoring the pilot project's technical and energetic performance as well as user acceptance. The efficiency of the system has since been enhanced to maximise extraction and storage of heat and minimise auxiliary power consumption required for operating the system, thus also making a net energy gain on the balance sheet. In the frame of this optimisation, the noise level of control valves and pumps was also improved. Directly in front of the façade and when located in the loggias, you can hear a slight "bubbling" noise that most residents have judged as being positive. By contrast, façade operations cannot be heard in the interior spaces of the passive house. In the loggias, where the bioreactors partially overlap the glazed balustrades, residents can get into direct touch with the bio-responsive façade elements. In the shade, protected from the wind and out of sight, they can watch the air bubbles rising.

While for the first time the building services system at »BIQ« converts, exchanges and stores the solar thermal heat generated by the bioreactors, or feeds it into the heating system and puts it at the users' disposal, the biomass is currently not exploited. Several ongoing research projects are focusing on how to develop an according value creation chain. They investigate processes in which high-quality microalgae components such as vitamins, amino and fatty acids, which are also much sought-after by pharmaceutical and food industries, could be separated from the rest of the biomass before it is used to supply energy. Other research work deals with the integration of the "SolarLeaf" façade into the primary façade of a building and covering the upper zones of the reactors with thin-layered PV modules in order to directly generate electricity in addition to biomass and heat. In this context, various variations to design such hybrid modules are compiled as a "kit of parts« for architects and designers, to allow project specific adaption of by integrating translucent, printed and coloured textures and interlayers.

Die Entwicklungsarbeit resultierte in einem außen liegenden Ve schattungssystem aus geschosshohen Glaslamellen mit integrierte Photobioreaktoren und solarthermischem Absorber. Die Lamelle sind auf ihrer Vertikalachse drehbar gelagert und lassen sich so de Sonnenstand nachführen. Alle Leitungen, etwa für die Luftzufu sowie für den Zu- und Abfluss der wässrigen Algenlösung, sind i Rahmen des Elements integriert. Jedes Fassadenelement bestel aus vier Glasscheiben. Sie umgeben einen zentralen, 18 mm breite Hohlraum, der pro Element bis zu 24 L Algenlösung fasst. Die Sche ben sind linienförmig entlang ihres Randes mechanisch durch eine Rahmen aus eloxierten Aluminiumstrangpressprofilen gelagert. A Außenscheibe des Elements fungiert ein aus Weißglas hergestellte Verbundsicherheitsglas mit einer Deckscheibe aus einem reflektion armen Gussglas, um die solaren Einträge zu maximieren.

DIE WELTWEIT ERSTE ANWENDUNG AM GEBÄUDE – DAS „BIQ" IN HAMBURG

Das viergeschossige Wohnhaus „BIQ" in Hamburg enthält 129 El mente der Algenfassade, die eine Nettooberfläche von rund 200 r bedecken. Die Algenfassade wurde als Sekundärstruktur vor d Südwest- und Südostfassade installiert. Jedes Fassadeneleme misst 2,50m x 0,70m; geschossweise sind die Paneele zu eine geschlossenen Wasserkreislauf verbunden und an den zentrale Technikraum im Erdgeschoss angebunden. Das zentrale Gebäud managementsystem überwacht die Zu- und Abflüsse jedes dies Cluster, die Nährstoffversorgung und die „Algenernte" an d Schnittstelle zur Gebäudetechnik. Auch der Algengehalt und di Temperatur der Lösung werden an dieser Stelle überprüft. Die Wä me, die durch den solarthermischen Effekt in den Bioreaktoren er steht, muss über das gesamte System verteilt werden, um desse Überhitzung zu vermeiden. Um eine gleich bleibende Energieerze gung zu gewährleisten, wird die Systemtemperatur unter 40°C g halten. Ein Wärmetauscher führt überschüssige Wärme aus de System ab; diese wird dann entweder direkt zur Warmwasserber tung genutzt – bei Bedarf unterstützt von einer Wärmepumpe oder über geothermische Sonden im Erdboden gespeichert.

Die Algenbiomasse, geschätzt etwa 15 Gramm Trockenmasse pr Quadratmeter Fassade und Tag, wird kontinuierlich oder in Schübe „geerntet". Die Ernte erfolgt durch „Flotation" in einem zylindri schen Behälter, in dem durch eingeführte Druckluft die Algen vo automatisch aufgeschäumt und abgeschöpft werden.

Bei der in Hamburg realisierten Pilotanlage des „BIQ" entsprici das „Biomasse-Potential" etwa 30 kWh je Quadratmeter Fassad und Jahr und der solare Wärmegewinn rund 150 kWh/m²a. Insg samt reduziert die Algenfassade den CO_2-Ausstoß des Gebäude um rund sechs Tonnen pro Jahr; zusätzlich absorbiert die Biomass 2,5 Tonnen CO_2 jährlich aus dem zugeführten Rauchgas.

WEITERENTWICKLUNGEN UND AUSBLICK

Seit der Inbetriebnahme des Gebäudes im April 2013 läuft ein u fangreiches Monitoring-Programm, das von den Partnern Aru SSC und Colt in Kooperation mit der HafenCity Universität Hamburg durchgeführt und von der Forschungsinitiative „Zukun Bau" gefördert wird. Das Monitoring erfasst sowohl die techr sche als auch die energetische Leistungsfähigkeit sowie die Nutze akzeptanz des Pilotprojektes. Seit Inbetriebnahme konnte die Ef zienz der Anlage soweit verbessert werden, dass sowohl die Au kopplung und Speicherung von Wärme optimiert als auch der f den Betrieb der Anlage erforderliche Hilfsstrom minimiert wurd so dass in der Bilanz die Anlage einen Nettoenergiegewinn prod ziert. Im Rahmen der Optimierung wurden auch die Steuerung ventile und die Pumpen schallakustisch optimiert. Direkt an d Fassade und an den Loggien ist ein leichtes „Blubbern" wahrz nehmen, das von den Bewohnern der Einheiten als durchweg p sitiv bewertet wird. In den Innenräumen des Passivhauses dageg ist der Betrieb der Fassade akustisch nicht wahrzunehmen. A den Loggien, wo sich die Bioreaktoren zum Teil vor die gläsern Brüstungen schieben, treten die Bewohner an warmen Tagen dire in Kontakt mit den bio-adaptiven Fassadenelementen. Hier könn

sum up, the bio-responsive façade aims to create synergies by connecting different systems (i.e. building services engineering, energy and heat distribution, various different water circulations, the food chain, etc.). Early co-operation between designers, contractors and industry is the key to successfully introducing photobioreactors on a larger scale in the future. The technology tested on IQ« will benefit from enhanced inter-disciplinary collaboration in the areas of environmental and climate technology, façade engineering, structural design, materials science and engineering, computer-supported simulation and building automation. Alongside continued close co-operation between architects and engineers, a holistic understanding of the advantages of the system for the building, users and environment will be crucial for future success.

sie wind- und sichtgeschützt im Halbschatten den visuellen Effekten der aufsteigenden Luftblasen folgen.

Während am „BIQ" erstmals die solarthermisch erzeugte Wärme der Bioreaktoren durch die Gebäudetechnik ausgekoppelt, transportiert, gespeichert und als Warmwasser bzw. durch den Heizkreislauf den Nutzern zur Verfügung gestellt wird, wird die Biomasse nicht direkt am Gebäude verwertet. Es laufen zurzeit Forschungsprojekte, um eine entsprechende Wertschöpfungskette aufzubauen. Dabei geht es um Verfahren, hochwertige Mikroalgen-Bestandteile wie Vitamine, Amino- und Fettsäuren, begehrt sowohl von Pharmaunternehmen als auch von der Lebensmittelindustrie, herauszulösen, bevor die übrige Biomasse der energetischen Verwertung zugeführt werden kann. Weitere Entwicklungsarbeiten zielen auf die Integration der „SolarLeaf" Fassade in die Primärfassade des Gebäudes und die Belegung der Kopfbereiche der Reaktoren mit „Dünnschicht-PV-Modulen" ab, um neben Wärme und Biomasse auch direkt Strom erzeugen zu können. In diesem Zusammenhang werden auch die Gestaltungsmöglichkeiten solcher Hybridmodule für Architekten und Planer als „Baukasten" zusammengestellt – durch die Integration von transluzenten, bedruckten und farbigen Beschichtungen und Zwischenschichten kann die architektonische Wirkung der Elemente projektspezifisch angepasst werden.

Zusammenfassend zielt die bio-adaptive Fassade darauf ab, Synergien durch Verknüpfung unterschiedlicher Systeme (d.h. Gebäudetechnik, Energie- und Wärmeverteilung, unterschiedliche Wasserkreisläufe, Nahrungsmittelkette) zu bilden. Schlüssel einer erfolgreichen Einführung von Photobioreaktoren in größerem Maßstab wird künftig die frühzeitige Zusammenarbeit zwischen Planern, Bauherren und der Industrie sein. Die am „BIQ" erprobte Technologie profitiert von starker interdisziplinärer Zusammenarbeit in den Bereichen der Umwelt- und Klimatechnik, der Fassadentechnik, Tragwerksplanung, Materialtechnologie, rechnergestützter Simulation und Gebäudeautomation. Am wichtigsten für den weiteren Erfolg wird ein ganzheitliches Verständnis der Vorteile des Systems für Gebäude, Nutzer und Umwelt sein – bei weiterhin enger Kooperation von Architekten und Fachplanern.

☐ ENTWURF & PLANUNG

25

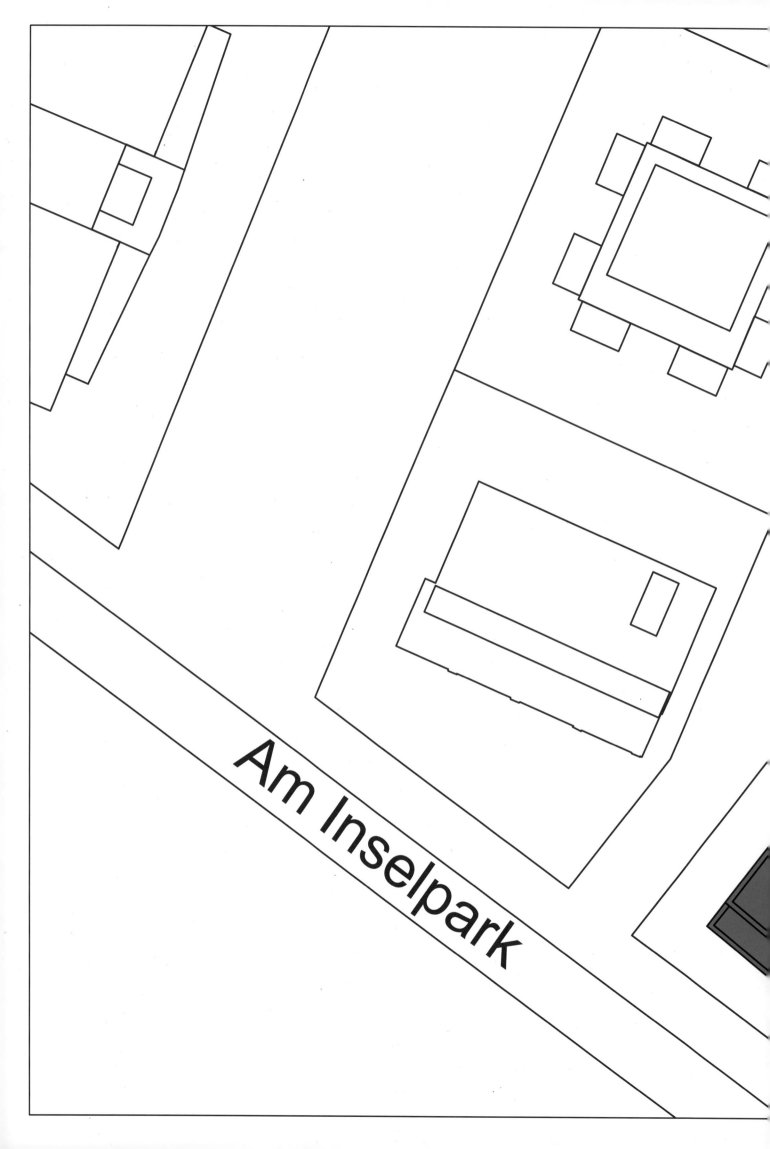

Am Inselpark

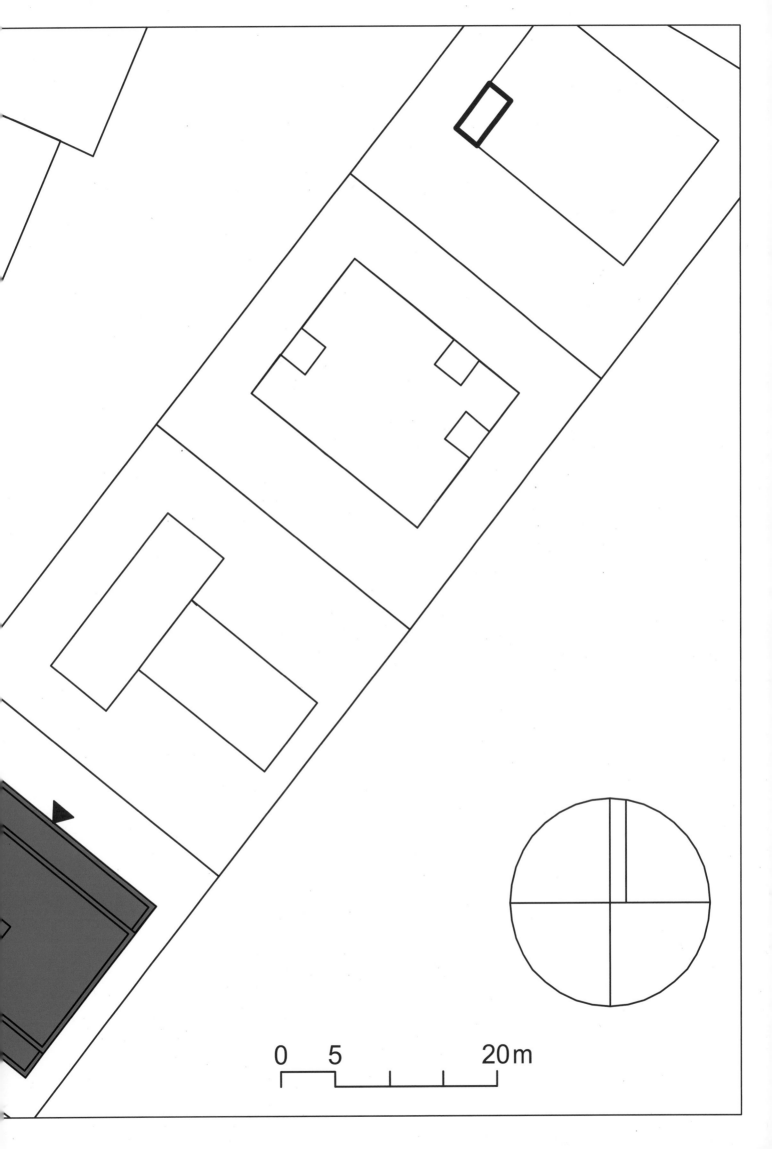

0 5 20m

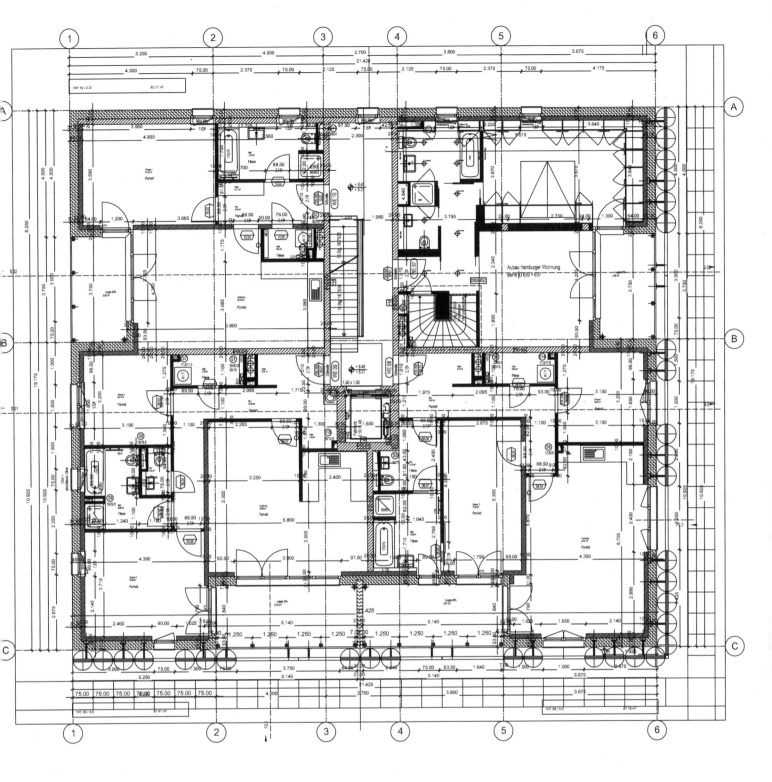

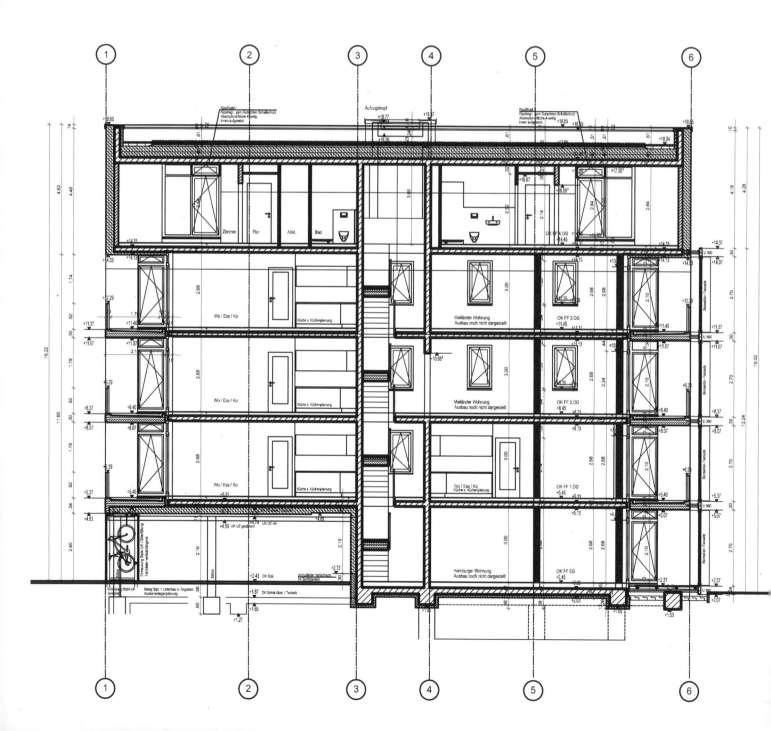

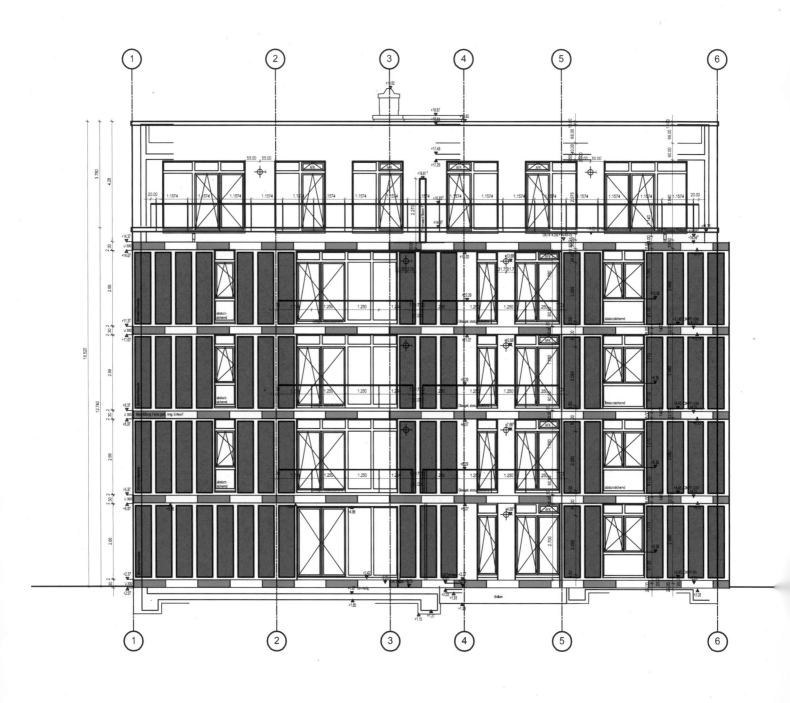

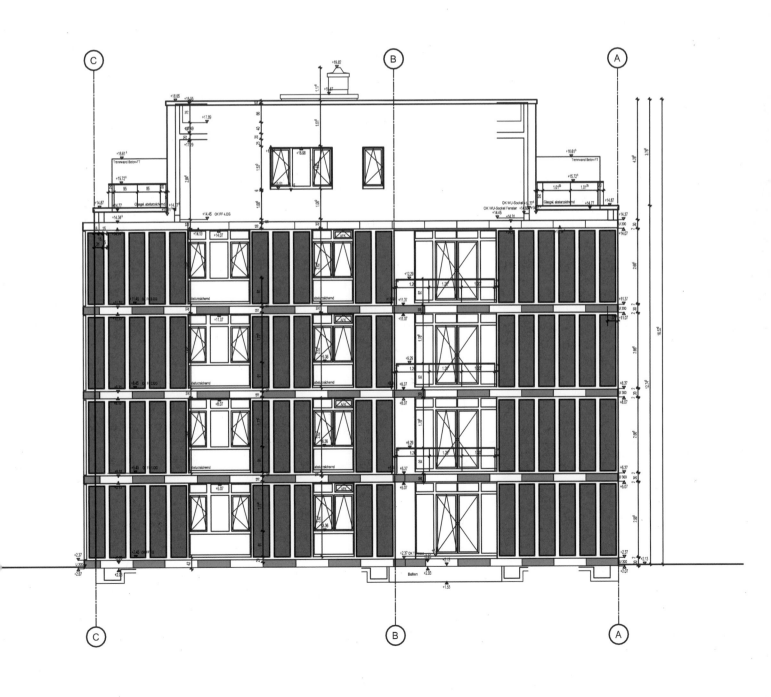

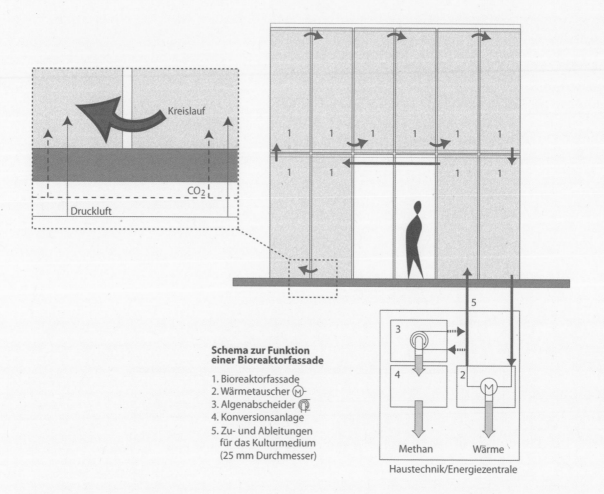

Kreislauf

CO$_2$

Druckluft

**Schema zur Funktion
einer Bioreaktorfassade**

1. Bioreaktorfassade
2. Wärmetauscher
3. Algenabscheider
4. Konversionsanlage
5. Zu- und Ableitungen
   für das Kulturmedium
   (25 mm Durchmesser)

Methan   Wärme

Haustechnik/Energiezentrale

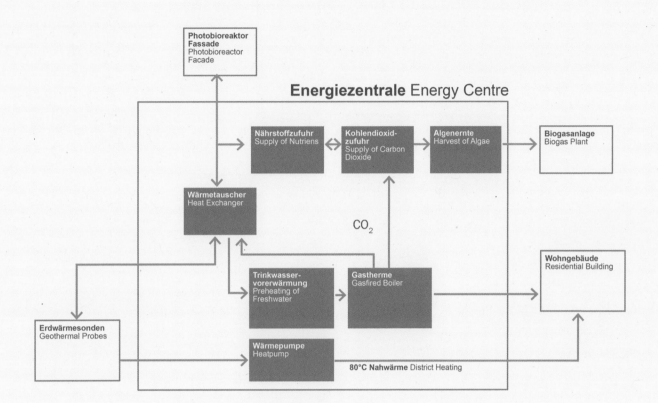

Energiezentrale Energy Centre

Photobioreaktor
Fassade
Photobioreactor
Facade

Nährstoffzufuhr
Supply of Nutriens

**Kohlendioxid-
zufuhr**
Supply of Carbon
Dioxide

Algenernte
Harvest of Algae

Biogasanlage
Biogas Plant

Wärmetauscher
Heat Exchanger

CO_2

**Trinkwasser-
vorerwärmung**
Preheating of
Freshwater

Gastherme
Gasfired Boiler

Wohngebäude
Residential Building

Erdwärmesonden
Geothermal Probes

Wärmepumpe
Heatpump

80°C Nahwärme District Heating

Anschlüsse der Photobioreaktor Fassade
Connections of the Photobioreactive Facade

Überlaufsensor
Overflowsensor

Zulauf Sprühdüse
Inlet Spray Nozzle

Zulauf Druckluft 1
Inlet Compressed Air

Zulauf Druckluft 2
Inlet Compressed Air

Zulauf Medium
Inlet Medium

Ablauf Medium
Output Medium

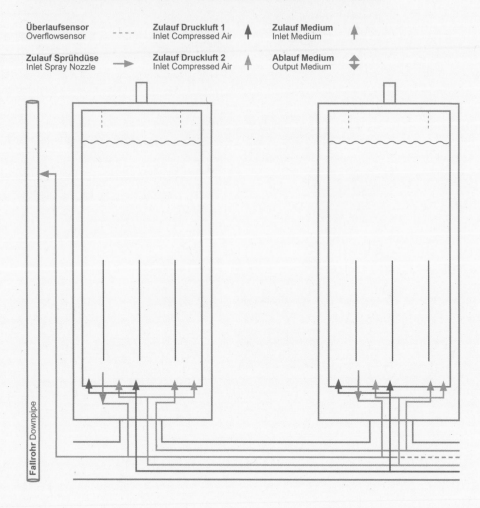

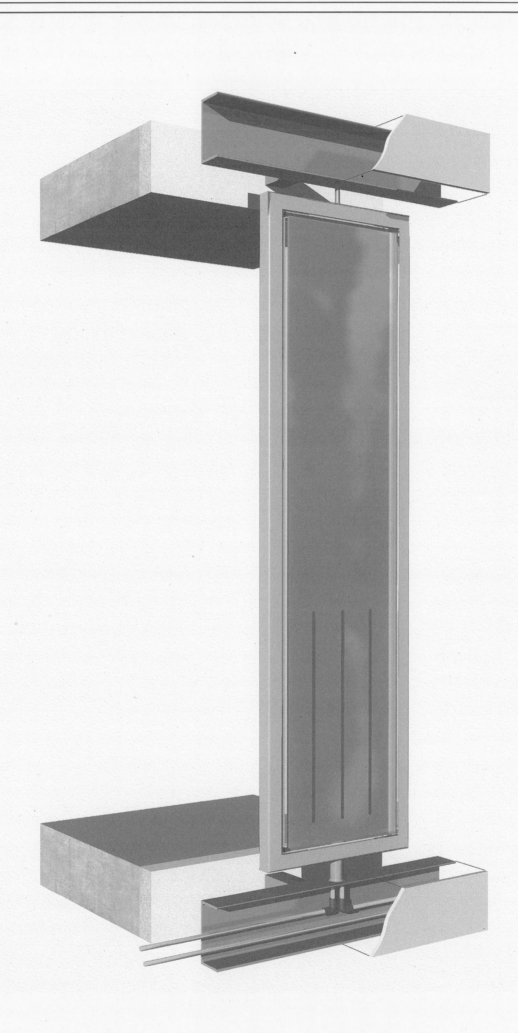

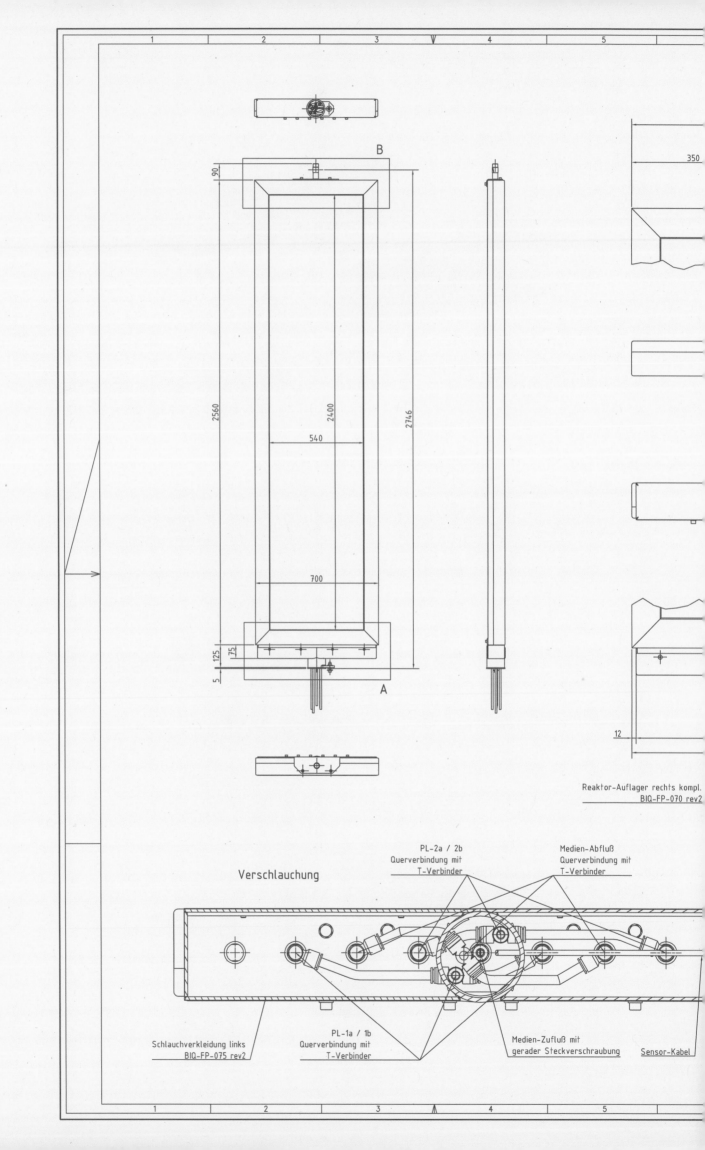

B

2560
2400
540
2746
700
125
75
5

A

350

12

Reaktor-Auflager rechts kompl.
BIQ-FP-070 rev2

Verschlauchung

PL-2a / 2b
Querverbindung mit
T-Verbinder

Medien-Abfluß
Querverbindung mit
T-Verbinder

Schlauchverkleidung links
BIQ-FP-075 rev2

PL-1a / 1b
Querverbindung mit
T-Verbinder

Medien-Zufluß mit
gerader Steckverschraubung

Sensor-Kabel

1   2   3   4   5

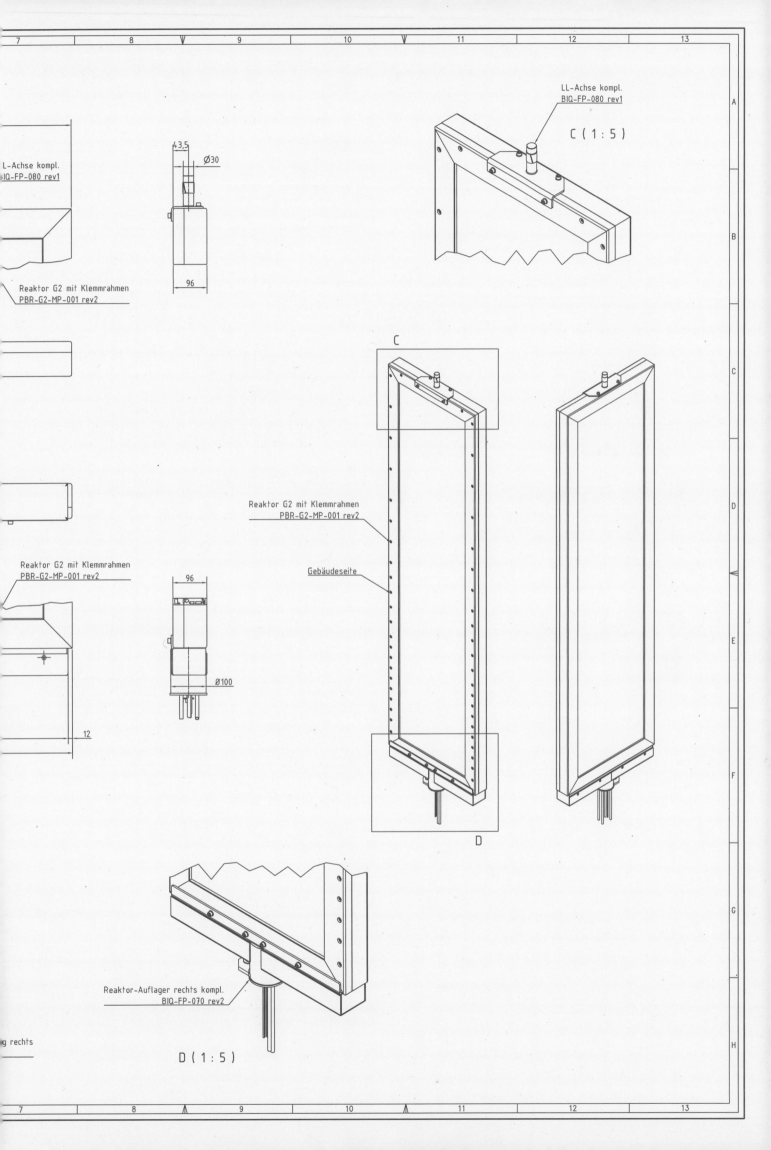

LL-Achse kompl.
BIQ-FP-080 rev1

C (1 : 5)

43,5
Ø30
96

L-Achse kompl.
IQ-FP-080 rev1

Reaktor G2 mit Klemmrahmen
PBR-G2-MP-001 rev2

C

Reaktor G2 mit Klemmrahmen
PBR-G2-MP-001 rev2

Reaktor G2 mit Klemmrahmen
PBR-G2-MP-001 rev2

Gebäudeseite

96

Ø100

12

D

Reaktor-Auflager rechts kompl.
BIQ-FP-070 rev2

g rechts

D (1 : 5)

7   8   9   10   11   12   13
A   B   C   D   E   F   G   H

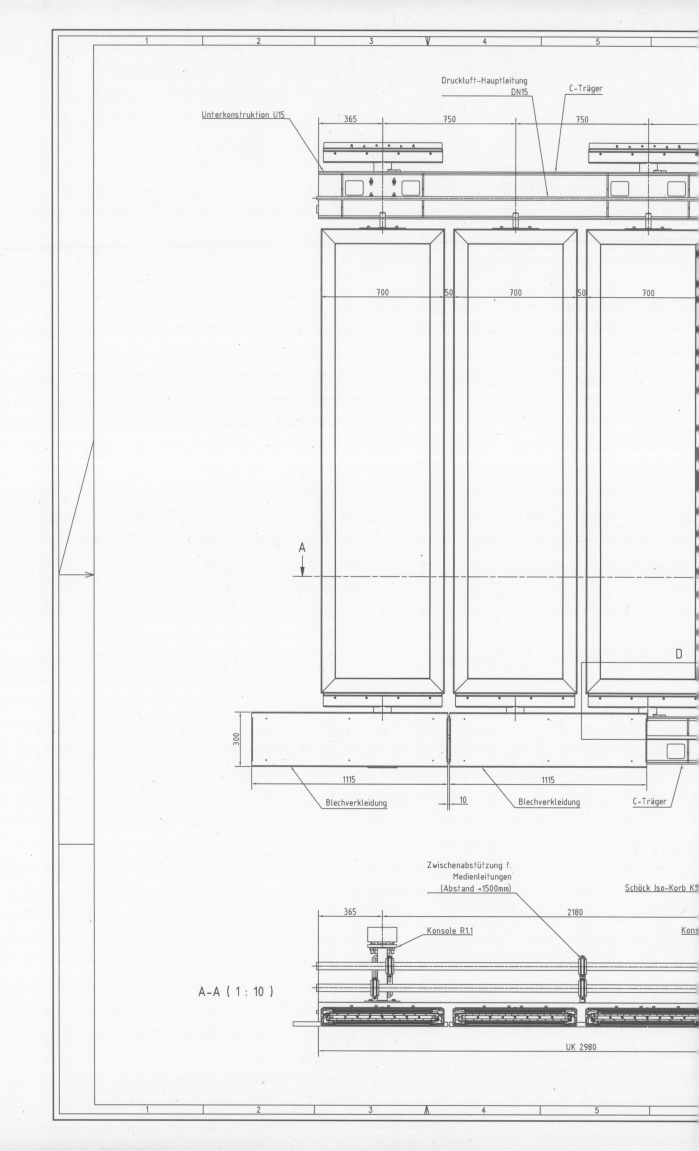

Unterkonstruktion U15

Druckluft-Hauptleitung
DN15

C-Träger

365   750   750

700   50   700   50   700

A

D

300

1115   1115

Blechverkleidung   10   Blechverkleidung   C-Träger

Zwischenabstützung f.
Medienleitungen
(Abstand <1500mm)

Schöck Iso-Korb K?

365   2180   Kons

Konsole R1.1

A-A (1 : 10)

UK 2980

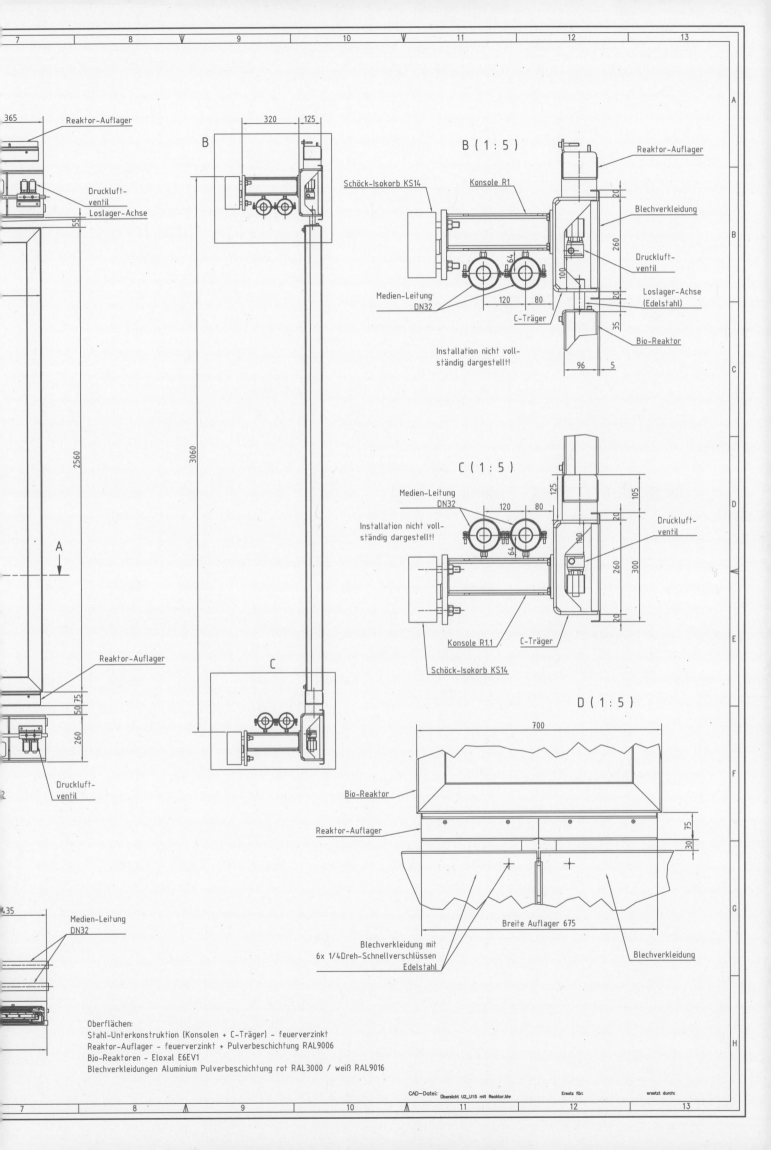

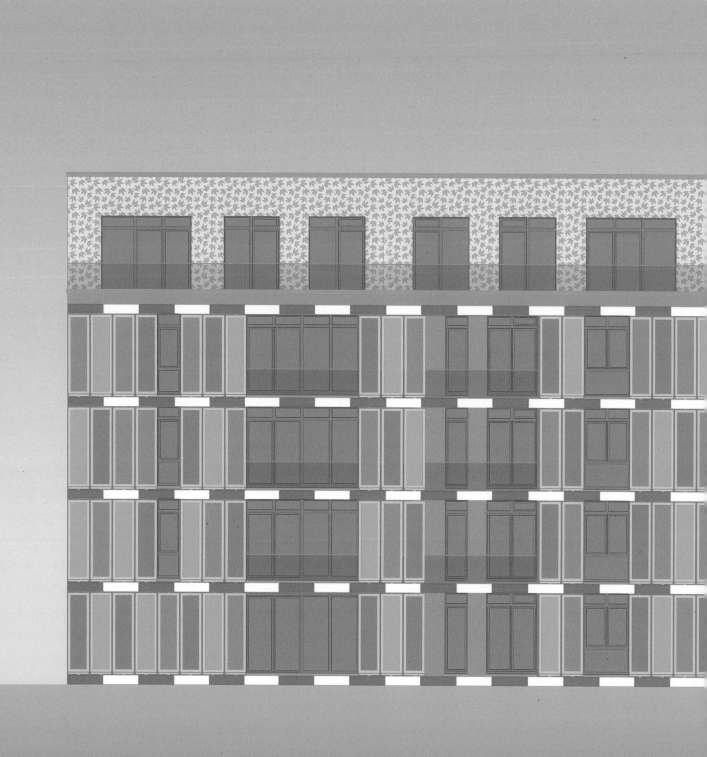

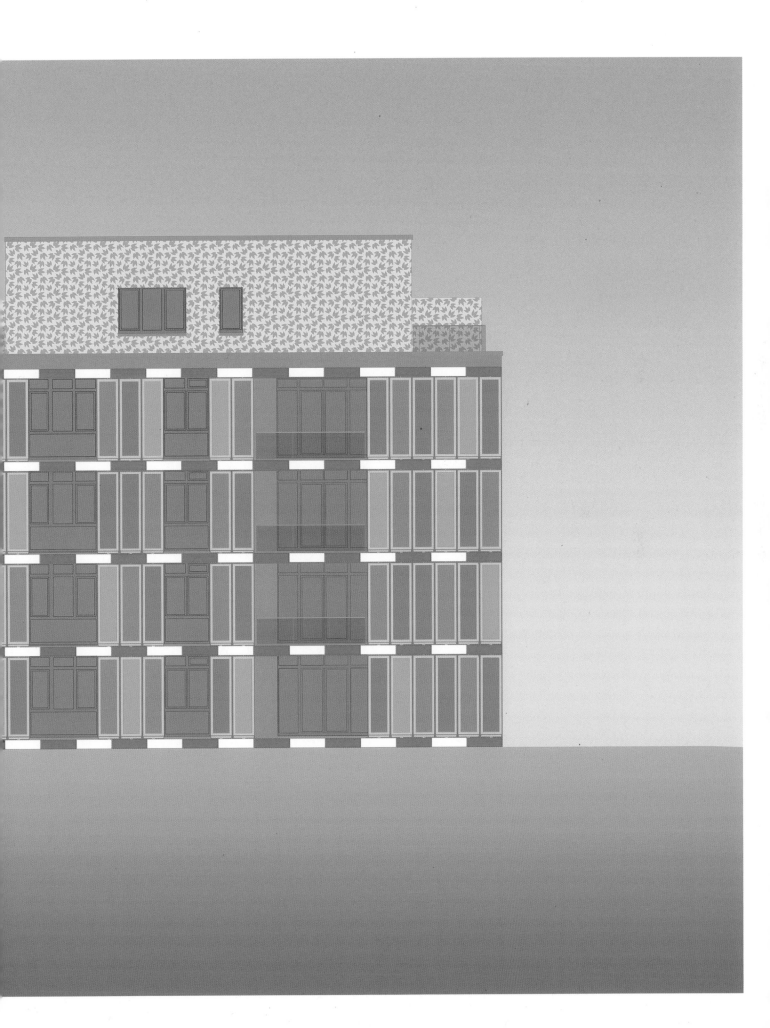

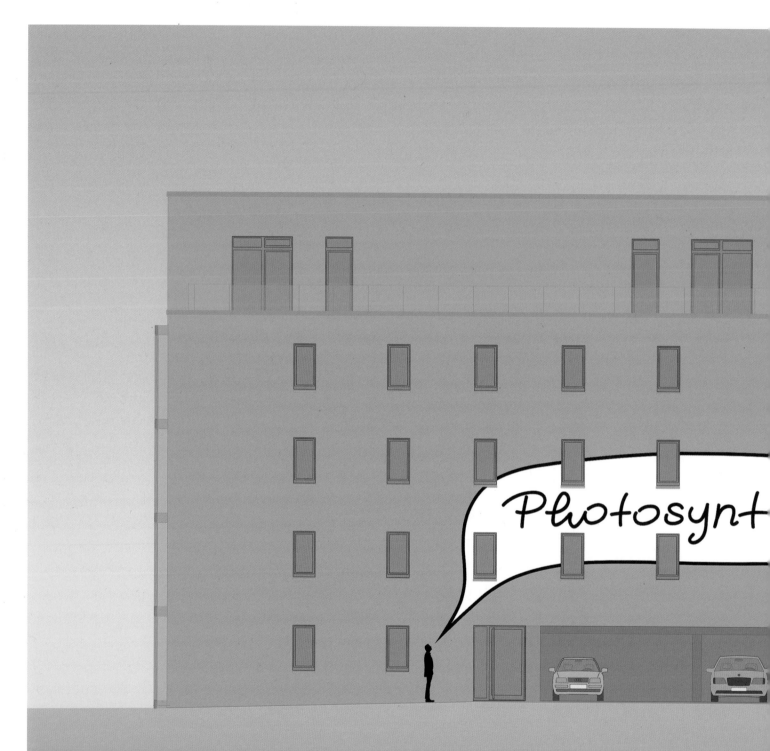

◻ FOTOESSAY PAUL OTT

☐ DIE HAMBURGER WOHNUNG (EG)

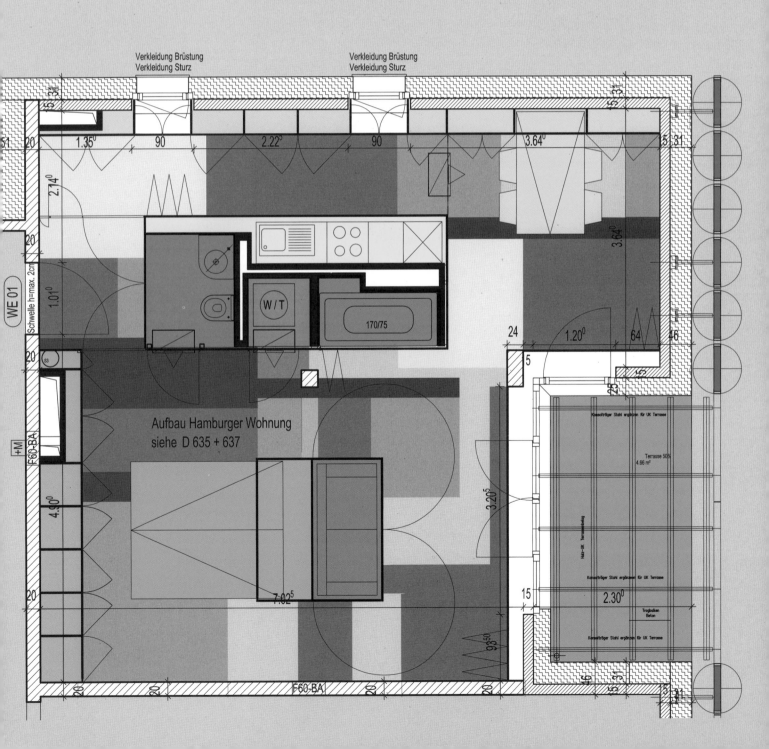

Verkleidung Brüstung
Verkleidung Sturz

Verkleidung Brüstung
Verkleidung Sturz

WE 01

Schwelle h=max. 2cm

+M

F60-BA

S3

1.35⁰   90   2.22⁵   90   3.64⁰

2.14⁰

1.01⁰

4.90⁰

20

20

20

20

20

20

51   20

15.31

15.31

3.64⁰

W / T

170/75

Aufbau Hamburger Wohnung
siehe D 635 + 637

7.02⁵

24   1.20⁰   64   46

5

3.20⁵

Kesselträger Stahl ergänzen für UK Terrasse

Terrasse 50%
4.66 m²

Holz-UK Terrassenbelag

Kesselträger Stahl ergänzen für UK Terrasse

15   2.30⁰

Trogbalken
Beton

Kesselträger Stahl ergänzen für UK Terrasse

9.50⁰

46   15.31   5.31

F60-BA

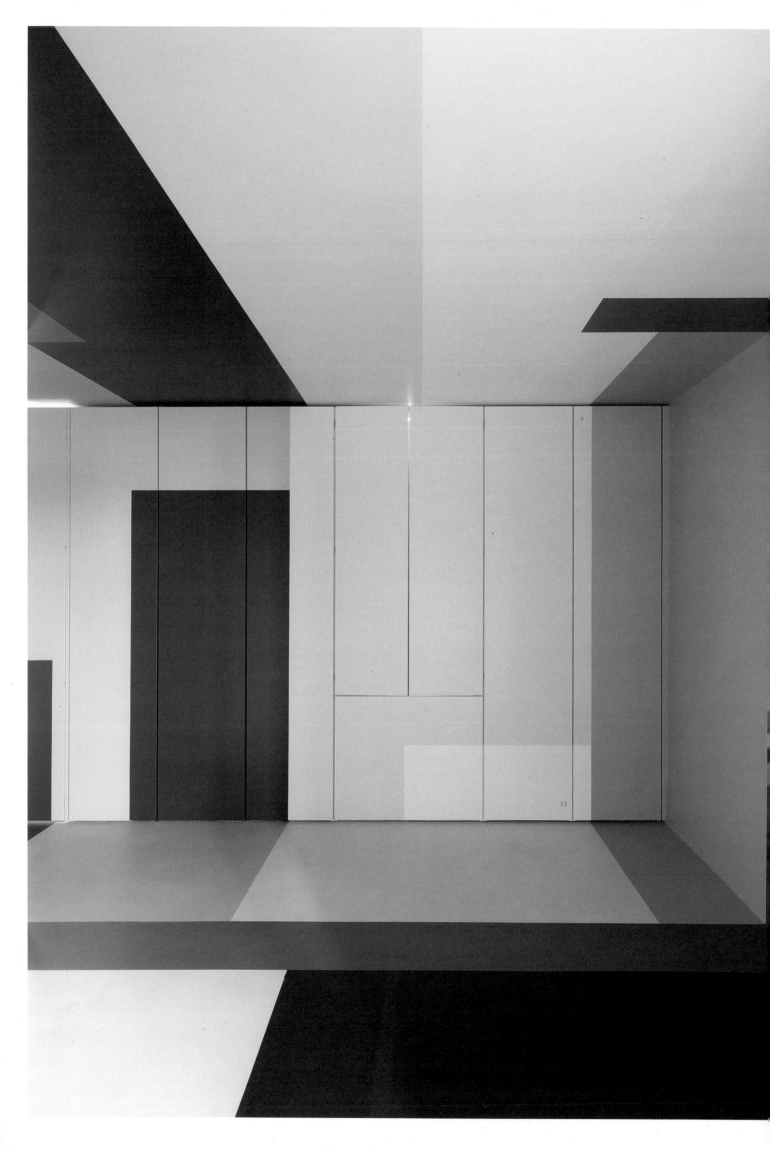

■ THE MILAN APARTMENT (2F)

□ DIE MAILÄNDER WOHNUNG (2.OG)

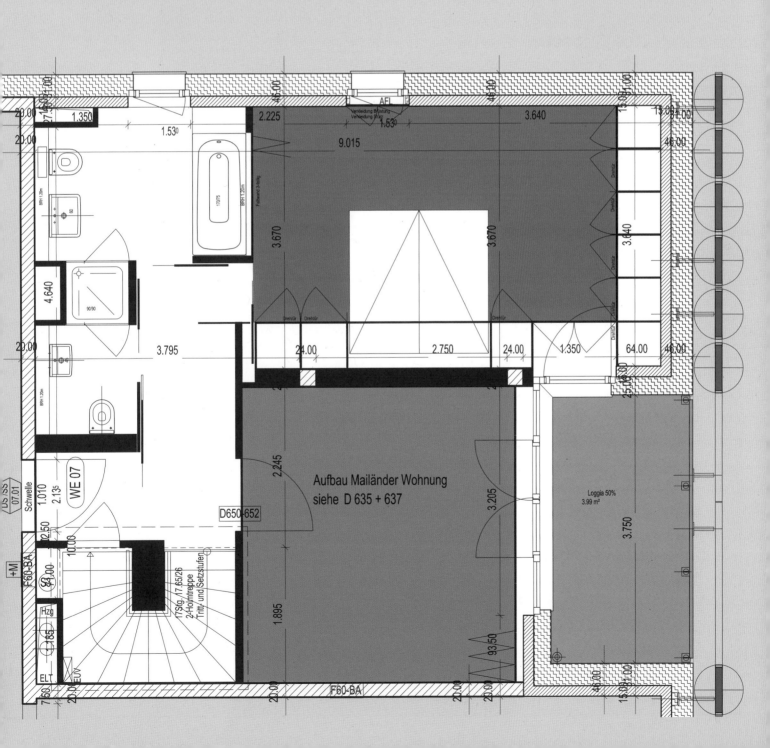

Aufbau Mailänder Wohnung
siehe D 635 + 637

WE 07

D650-652

Loggia 50%
3.99 m²

The Luncheon
on the Grass

Invisible Cities

■ THE MILAN APARTMENT (3F)

☐ DIE MAILÄNDER WOHNUNG (3.OG)

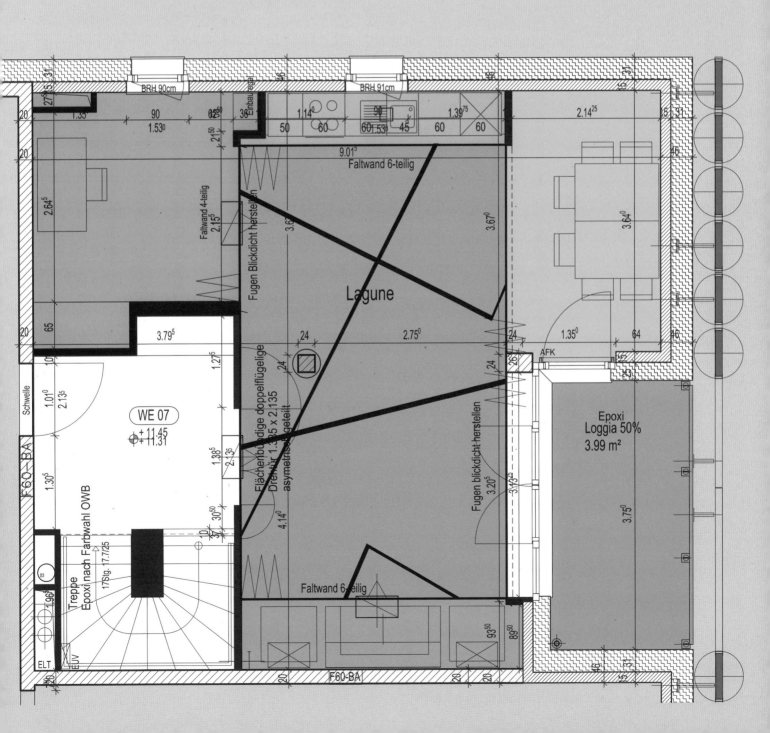

BRH 90cm

BRH 91cm

Einbauregal

Faltwand 6-teilig

Faltwand 4-teilig

Fugen Blickdicht herstellen

Lagune

Flächenbündige doppelflügelige
Drehtür 1.385 x 2.135
asymetrisch geteilt

Fugen blickdicht herstellen

Epoxi
Loggia 50%
3.99 m²

WE 07
+ 11.45
+ 11.31

Schwelle

Treppe
Epoxi nach Farbwahl OWB
17Stg. 17.7/25

ELT

EUV

F60-BA

AFK

Faltwand 6-teilig

F60-BA

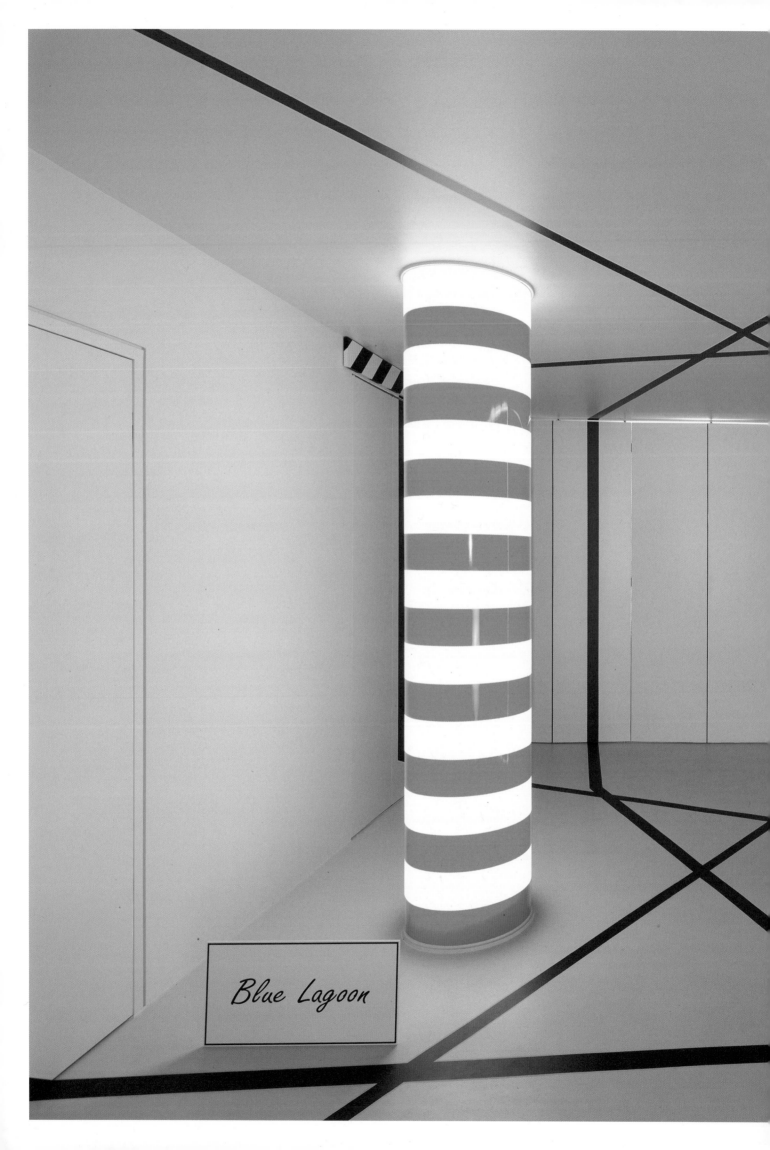

Blue Lagoon

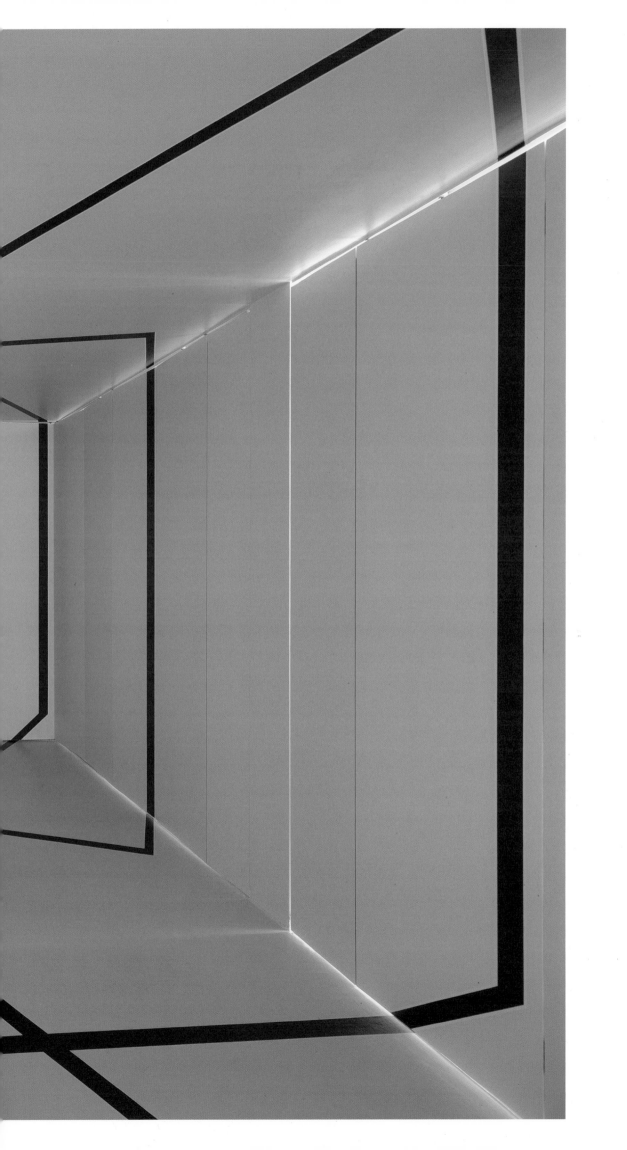

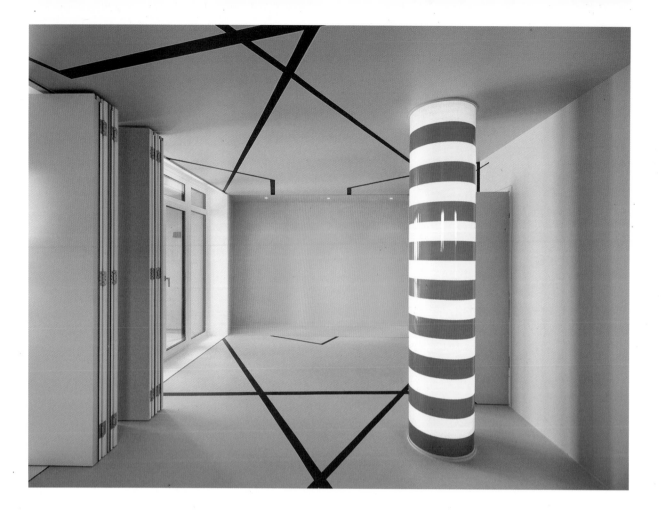

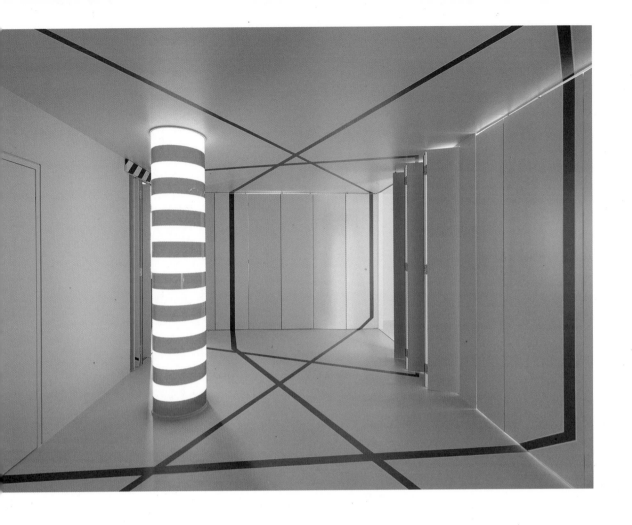

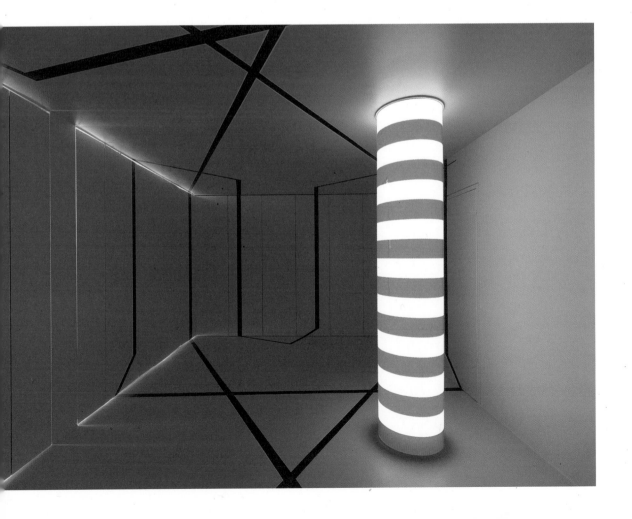